a dress for anna

The Story Of The Redemption
Of The Life Of A Ukrainian Orphan

deborah j. amend

CSS Publishing Company, Inc., Lima, Ohio

a dress
for anna

The Story Of The Redemption
Of The Life Of A Ukrainian Orphan

deborah j. amend

A DRESS FOR ANNA

Published by CSS Publishing Company, Inc., Lima, Ohio 45804.

14   13   12   11   10   09   7   6   5   4   3   2   1

Library of Congress Cataloging-in-Publication Data

Amend, Deborah.
    A dress for Anna : the story of the redemption of the life of a Ukrainian orphan / Deborah Amend. — 1st ed.
        p. cm.
    ISBN 0-7880-2632-1 (Perfect bound : alk. paper)
    1. Adoptive parents—United States—Biography. 2. Intercountry adoption—United States. 3. Intercountry adoption—Ukraine. 4. Adoption—Religious aspects—Christianity. 5. Adopted children—Ukraine. I. Title.
    HV875.5.A437 2009
    362.734092—dc22

                                                                2009009028

ISBN-13: 978-0-7880-2632-4
ISBN-10: 0-7880-2632-1   PRINTED IN USA

For Anna
Gentle Warrior, Loving Daughter,
Beautiful Girl

Instead of the thorn bush will grow the pine tree, and instead of briers the sweet myrtle will grow. This will be for the LORD's renown, for an everlasting sign, which will not be destroyed.
— Isaiah 55:13 (NIV)

For every child who waits for
their Mama and Papa to come for them

"For I know the plans I have for you," declares the Lord, "Plans to prosper you, not to harm you, plans to give you a hope and a future."
— Jeremiah 29:11 (NIV)

Acknowledgments

There are so many people to thank when it comes to the miracle of not only this book, but the story of our family, that this page is only a start ...

Thank you to my husband, Rob, who made this book a reality. Thank you for your trust in me when I said that God was calling us to do some crazy things. Thank you for your faithfulness to God and your willingness to live uncomfortably. Thank you for always loving me like Christ loves the church, and know that never a day goes by that I do not thank God for the blessing of our marriage. It's been an adventure!

Thank you to my children: Ben, Justin, Anna, Saya, and Aly for being who they are and blessing my life with love, joy, and a lot of really good company. Each of you is a precious treasure from heaven. I'm thankful that God made me your mom.

Thank you to Luba, and all the ladies at the Baby House, who loved and prayed for Anna before we ever knew her. You are truly the hands and feet of God, bringing his love to children so very dear to his heart.

Thank you to Christian Adoptive Families for the support over the years, especially Melinda Hickman and Pam Blair, who have shared my passion for helping other families bring home their children. I am thankful for your friendship and lives and that God has called us to serve together.

Thank you to Kevin and Ginger Mitchell and my parents for caring for our children left behind as we traveled to redeem those who had been lost.

And thank you to Jesus Christ who gave up all in order to adopt me into his family.

Table Of Contents

Prologue

He is no fool who gives what he cannot keep to gain what he cannot lose. — Jim Elliott

Do not store up for yourselves treasures on earth, where moth and rust destroy, and where thieves break in and steal. But store up for yourselves treasures in heaven, where moth and rust do not destroy, and where thieves do not break in and steal. For where your treasure is, there your heart will be also.
— Matthew 6:19-21 (NIV)

Whoever finds his life will lose it, and whoever loses his life for my sake will find it.
— Matthew 10:39 (NIV)

Elena Ivanova* walked briskly down the quiet street. Though the sun shone brightly, the air was chilly. She pulled her coat tightly across her waist and tightened the scarf that covered her short, brown hair. Her workbag hung at her elbow, bouncing off her hip as her heel hit the ground. Chickens scampered about her feet as she made her way around the large potholes in the road, and cherry trees, just starting to bud, towered above her head, lining the street leading up to the orphanage. As she approached the rusting wrought iron gates that marked the edge of the orphanage property, she could hear the voices of the children drifting out through the cold morning air.

For years, she had made this walk. Although her work was difficult, she was often not paid for it. If a government has no money, then it follows that they are not able to pay their employees. It matters not how important or difficult that work might be. Over these many years she, and her coworkers, had cared for more children than she could keep track of. Yet, she had loved them all. Some had had the good fortune of being adopted, but most had simply moved on to another orphanage ... a very bleak future ahead of them.

When she entered the orphanage, she walked straight to the section that housed her *groupa* — ten infants that were placed in the care of her and several other women. She stopped outside the nursery to set down her belongings, took down a white robe, designed to protect her from the babies' messes, and tied it tightly around her waist.

"Elena," the director called from down the hallway, "there is a new girl in your group. She's in the third crib. Her name is Halyna."

Elena walked into the nursery, eager to meet her new charge. She peered over the edge of crib three. There lay a tiny baby, swaddled tightly, sleeping peacefully. Long, dark eyelashes fringed the child's eyes and contrasted with beautiful honey-colored hair. She had a gentle slope to her nose and perfect doll-like lips.

"Beautiful ..." Elena whispered as she gently picked her up to hold her as she prayed over her. But before she could start her prayer, she was distracted by something. Over the years Elena Ivanova had lifted many babies out of cribs and something about this child felt different.

As Elena began to unwrap the swaddling, Halyna's eyelids fluttered opened and a tiny smile crossed her face. The beauty of this tiny baby was amazing. She seemed so perfect, until Elena unwrapped the final layer of blanket. A gasp slipped from her lips

12

as she first saw the baby's physical handicaps. Gently, she reswaddled Halyna, and held the child tightly, next to her heart.

Envisioning the bleak future that life in the orphanage system held for this precious girl, she prayed to God, the first of many prayers on behalf of this child.

"Please, God, send a family for Halyna ... please ... one from a country where she can get medical care and have hope ... please send her a family from America ... a family that will love her."

That spring morning, God heard that prayer.

Far across the Atlantic Ocean, not long after that first prayer for the future of Halyna was offered, God set that plan in motion, and my family and I were unsuspecting players.

There were two men standing at the podium at the front of the sanctuary of our church. One man was delivering a message from a church in Ukraine; the other man was translating for him.

"It is difficult to finish the construction of the church when we are forced to replace the wiring and construction materials that are often stolen. We add wiring and within days it is stolen. So, we move forward slowly."

It was difficult to imagine trying to complete such an enormous task as constructing a church building amid such poverty — people stealing the copper wiring from the building simply to sell it in order to buy bread. As I listened to them speak, I felt a great empathy for their situation.

But, I thought to myself, *what could I ever do to really help?*

The answer came several minutes later when our pastor explained the role that our church would play in helping our brothers and sisters in Ukraine.

"On Thanksgiving Sunday, we will give you an opportunity to pledge an amount of money to give to the Ukrainian church. This gives you time to pray and think about what God would have you give.... We will collect the money, in a special offering, the first week of January."

Although our own financial situation was far from affluent, I had been moved by the sermon that morning and really desired to give the Ukrainian church a gift that was big enough to make a difference in their budget. That afternoon, my husband, Rob, and I discussed the plan.

At that time, we had the option of earning money by keeping a phone line for a local business in our apartment. If the owner of the business was called from his office, calls were forwarded to our home, and we were paid to answer. Paid by the hour, the income (about $50 to $70 per week) was supplemental to what was in our budget.

"Why don't we just donate every other pay check to the church?" I asked Rob. "It's money that we didn't plan on anyway, so we won't even miss it."

He was agreeable to the plan and set an empty coffee can in that hallway intending to stick every other paycheck in it until the Sunday we would commit an amount to the church.

The first week that I answered phones with the intent of donating the money, I earned around $200. The next week was my week. I earned about $70. The following week for donations: $100. My week: $50. And so it continued until I had nearly $500 for the church in Ukraine. On Thanksgiving Sunday, I turned in my pledge card, elated by what God had provided.

However, it was not long before my promise to God wavered. That amount, for almost anyone, would be large, but for a stay-at-home mom whose husband was a full-time graduate student, that amount was enormous. My heart strongly desired to serve God, but my flesh, just as strongly, desired to serve me.

"I'll just deposit the money until it's time to offer it to God." I rationalized. "It's silly for the checks to just sit here on my desk. It makes more sense to have them in our checking account."

It was not long before I had deposited the checks, and subsequently, spent all of the money. For several days I justified what I was doing. We had very little money at the time, and I convinced myself that a family of four living on such a small income should never make that kind of donation to a church on the other side of the world. I told myself that there were enough people at church that could pick up the slack and that my money was not needed.

However, in my heart, I knew. I knew that I had made a promise to God — had given that money to him — and then took it back pretending that none of it had ever happened. My conscience nagged me, and within days, I knew that I would need to repent. After my repentance, we needed a new plan.

"I promised that money to God," I told Rob. "We have to deliver."

"I agree," he replied. "So we scrimp and pinch and save everything we can until the first Sunday in January."

And we did. With Christmas approaching it was not an easy task, but any time I considered giving up, I thought about the other alternative: not delivering what I had promised. It was much easier to live with slighted means than it would be to live with the guilt of breaking a promise to Jesus.

About a week into our scrimping and pinching, we received a surprise. A check arrived in the mail from our health insurance company. Somehow, over the course of the year, we had accidentally overpaid our premiums — by exactly the same amount of money that I had promised God. It was obviously God's provision for our repentance and obedience.

Almost instantly, though, I was tempted to spend the money again. Realizing that I needed to move the money along as quickly as possible, I wrote the check to the church the moment we deposited the insurance check in the bank. I held the check in my purse until the Sunday that the offering was collected.

Still, though, I was attached to the money, and I struggled with giving so much. However, as the offering plate came near, I began to feel peace. At the moment that I placed the envelope in the plate, I distinctly heard God's voice. It was clear in my mind, and I was certain it was him.

"Your obedience will not come back void."

Of course, I thought, *I know that this money will go much farther in Ukraine than it would at home.*

"No, not just that ..." he said. "*Your obedience* will not come back void."

15

That Sunday morning, I gave from my heart to God's work in Ukraine. And that Sunday morning, I believe, God began to set in motion the events that would lead to me receiving the best gift I could have ever been given in return for my obedience. I gave God a mere $500 to use in Ukraine. In return, God gave me a Ukrainian daughter.

---

*This name was created for a fictional retelling of Anna's arrival at the orphanage in Ukraine.

The Best-Laid Plans

The best-laid plans of mice and men often go awry.
— Adapted from Robert Burn's "To A Mouse"

In his heart a man plans his course, but the Lord determines his steps. — Proverbs 16:9 (NIV)

Many are the plans in a man's heart but it is the Lord's purpose that prevails. — Proverbs 19:21 (NIV)

It all started with a simple prayer.

"Tell me again why we're doing this?" I often asked Rob when we were at our wit's end with the adoption process.

"Because you asked him for his input," he would reply.

It was true. When most people want to have a baby, they just go ahead and participate in all the actions necessary to produce one! I, however, felt that I should ask God what his opinion on the matter was. I did not really expect an answer, I just wanted to cover all my bases before we added another child to our family.

"Lord, I want another baby — a girl would be nice. Is this in your plans for us?"

At the time I prayed this prayer, our family consisted of my husband, Rob, our two boys, Ben and Justin, and me. Rob was a full-time graduate student, and we both worked several part-time jobs. Our days were hectic, but I loved being a mommy and I enjoyed taking care of my boys.

Ben's birth would mark a dramatic change in my life, bringing me home to care for him rather than returning to my work as a inner city high school music teacher. The change in my daily routine was not the only difference. Until the arrival of Ben, I had been our family's main wage earner as Rob finished his schooling.

But daycare, nannies, or babysitting were not a part of the vision we had for our family, as we both believed that large amounts of time were necessary to build relationships. Believing that God was calling me to stay home with our new son, we took the first dramatic step of faith we ever took as a family. It was the practice step that led to us having the courage to take the leap of faith God would call us to several years later. Upon learning that Ben would arrive the following autumn, I did not renew my teaching contract for the next school year.

In the summer leading up to Ben's birth, we pieced together our income. Rob was a full-time student with a part-time job at the university he attended. I began teaching several piano students out of our apartment. We paid our insurance premiums out of pocket, gathered hand-me-down baby items, and waited for what God was going to do. As we waited, our money began to dwindle. I hoped for one big miraculous answer of provision, but instead, God slowly pieced things together for us.

Before long, I had a very small piano studio and a part-time teaching job at a local Christian elementary school. Together with Rob's income, it formed a small sum for us to live on, as long as we did not have to pay rent. With the end of the month looming ahead of us we were growing concerned about the following month's rent. Insurance premiums, medical costs due to the pregnancy, and food used all our money. So, we had no choice but to depend upon God. And, it was not long before he answered with a phone call.

"Hello," Rob answered into the phone. As I pondered how we would pay for our phone service, he continued his conversation.

"Interesting ..." Rob's eyebrows furrowed. "Let me take down the name and number and talk to Deb about it."

As he hung up the phone, he explained. The call had been from a long-time friend of the family.

"We have had a very unusual offer ... but I'm not sure...."

"Go on ..." I urged, frustrated at the slow pace he was using to reveal the information. I had hopes that this call was God's answer to our money situation.

"Well, there's someone who owns a funeral home. Apparently they have a position that has opened up and they are looking for a couple to fill it. They need caretakers to handle the property and answer phones. It's part-time, and the payment's a rent-free apartment."

That was just about the last thing that I expected to hear. It did not even cross my mind as a possibility of what I was about to hear. In fact, I was pretty sure that it was an offer that I didn't want to hear. Living with dead people?

However, God has an odd way of providing, and it was *free* ... so we called the number and set up an interview.

For the next few days, I imagined the funeral home and apartment. We realized that we had chosen a difficult path, and I didn't stop my full-time job in order to gain more comfort. I expected it to be hard but believed that the fruit we would get from investing our time in our family would outweigh the sacrifices that we made.

Still ... a *funeral home?*

Every time I pictured the building, it had a sort of mysterious yellow hue about it, with a sort of supernatural fog surrounding it. The owner, a creepy old man with a peculiar odor about him, stood in the doorway. The apartment, in my mind's eye, was small and dark. There was a tiny kitchen with a single light dangling from a duct-taped electrical cord. An occasional rodent would scamper across the floor.

Beyond the physical picture, I labored with a deeper issue: How in the world would I be able to sleep in a building that I shared with the deceased?

It was hardly my dream to live in a funeral home, but I was willing to accept any help God would offer and I knew that what I wanted was time to spend with my baby. As long as it was safe, warm, and comfortable, any odd odors or sights could be dealt with.

"It's temporary," I kept reminding myself.

I was quite surprised, then, when we located the funeral home for our interview. First of all, it was a large, old farmhouse. There was no yellow glow and certainly no mysterious fog. It had a large yard and was within walking distance of a shopping center. The building, in fact, was a beautiful historical landmark with the original house dating back to the Civil War.

As for the director, he was neither old nor odd smelling. He was approximately our age and had recently inherited the business from his father. In fact, the place was quite homey and friendly. After the interview, he gave us a tour of the apartment, which was located on the second story of the funeral home. It was more than twice as big as the apartment we were currently renting, far beyond what I could've ever imagined. There was an eat-in kitchen, a dining room, a large living room, and two large bedrooms. The previous caretakers had decorated with wallpaper and paint, and it had a very comfortable feel to it.

We drove home from the interview and started packing to move. I realized, then, that when God provides for his children, he does so lavishly. All we needed was a place to live. We were not looking to improve our living conditions but to simply find a way to pay for them. In his generosity, he provided that and much more.

One week after Ben's birth, we moved into the apartment. Despite my previous fears about sleeping with dead people, I slept more soundly than I had since Ben's birth. The first week of his life, living in a four-family apartment building, had been very stressful. Each night, I worried as he cried and screamed throughout the night that he was disturbing the neighbors. He could wail all he wanted at our new home, but would never (thank God!) wake our new neighbors!

The funeral home, then, became our home. We cleaned, maintained the yard, handled the phones, and helped host evening visitations. Ben grew, and was joined by a younger brother, Justin, a year and a half later. Over time, God blessed my piano studio and it grew into a large enough business that it supplemented our income very well.

The funeral home provided just the right setting for our family, and did so for years, until we purchased a home just about a year before we began our adoption journey. Our piano was kept in a visitation room, which could be opened up for recitals and classes, and made for a convenient setup for me to continue my work as a music teacher. Our family lived quite comfortably in our apartment. It was perfect provision for our family's needs, including needs that we had not foreseen when we first got the call.

While living there, many people often commented on how brave we were to live in such a place — a thought I found quite amusing. If God's promises are true, then what could possibly be so scary about living in a funeral home? It was a simple matter of trusting God and trusting that he provided that opportunity for us.

The issues with living there never centered on our deceased co-inhabitants. They centered upon our workload and our situation of living day-to-day by the hand of God. Although it brought us closer to him, it was not easy. After several years, we were very tired of maintaining so many responsibilities and not having any idea of what the future held.

Four years, two degrees (both earned by Rob), and two babies later, we were still living in that apartment. As Rob was just beginning his first full-time professional job, we were able to concentrate on future plans instead of just getting through the day. Ben and Justin, though, were happy, healthy, little boys who were very secure in our family and off to a great start in life. All the schooling and stress were behind us, and we were ready to start saving up for a house. And, I was preparing for what I hoped would be our first girl.

That is what led me, that summer day, to pray and seek God about having a baby. After I prayed, I waited. For several minutes there was complete silence, and then a thought that I did not want to hear came into my head.

"No."

That was it. Nothing else. I was certain that I had not heard correctly. Why would God not want us to have another baby? I thought that we were good parents, but maybe he didn't think so. I tried to convince myself that I heard incorrectly. But I had heard the answer so clearly that I knew it was from him. If children are a gift from God, what could this mean?

It took me several days to even get the courage up to pray again. Hearing "no" as an answer cut deep into my heart and felt as though it not only broke it, but ripped it into pieces. I couldn't even talk to God, and I certainly did not want to bring this up with any other person. His "no" felt like I was being told that I was a bad parent, that, when consulted, God made it clear we should stop where we were.

I thought through all the parenting mistakes that I had made. I thought about all the other mistakes that I had made. I filled my mind with so much information that I was certain I couldn't hear God if he even did try to speak again. It was the adult equivalent of a child sticking their fingers in their ears and talking so they can't hear what their parents are saying.

Finally, though, I knew that I needed to work through whatever God was trying to teach me. My heart was so disconcerted that I was willing to do whatever I needed to be at peace with him. Wanting to resolve this matter and trying to understand what I thought I heard, I tried again.

I prayed, and waited....

"No...."

"Again!" I raged at God, "What's this 'no' bit? I'm such a bad person? Such a bad parent? I know that we don't have a lot of money, but we can teach this child what is important...."

But before I could finish my ranting, God interrupted my thoughts and finished his.

"No ... adopt."

It seemed to be so clearly God's voice, and yet it just was not saying what I wanted it to say. I tried to persuade myself that it was simply my mind wondering, as it just did not make any sense. Adoption was something that couples did when infertility treatments didn't work, and although I didn't know much about adoption, what

I did know was that there were waiting lists of infertile couples who wanted to adopt. We were able to have babies, so there was no reason for us to adopt one.

The other thing that I knew about adoption was that it's expensive. We had no money. Obviously this could not have been the voice of God. I did my best to dismiss all thoughts about my prayer and adoption.

Despite my resolve to not think about it, I often heard the word "adopt" in my mind. There were visual reminders everywhere: Adopt-a-Highway, Adopt-an-Animal at the zoo, Adopt-a-Dog from the pound. Down the street from our home was a billboard advertising for foster parents. The evening news often showed a segment on a local child that was available for adoption through the county.

Even a trip to the library became an opportunity to think about adoption. As I pushed Justin's stroller to the children's section, I passed a small kiosk that held free bookmarks. I grabbed one as we walked by. I nearly fell over when I read it:

> *100 years from now it will not*
> *Matter what size my bank account was,*
> *What kind of clothes I wore, or what*
> *Kind of car I drove,*
> *But the world may be a different place*
> *because I was important in the life of a child.*
>
> *Interested in Adoption?*
>
> *We can help.*
> *Call Cincinnati Children's Home*

It seemed like the more I tried to stop thinking about it, the more I saw the words "adoption" and "orphan." It didn't take long for me to realize that even though we had a nice plan for our family, God had had a different plan and had been working on that plan for quite some time.

The Grand Plan

You shall know the truth, and the truth shall make you odd.... — Attributed to Flannery O'Connor

The angel of the Lord came and sat down under the oak in Ophrah that belonged to Joash the Abiezrite, where his son Gideon was threshing wheat in a winepress to keep it from the Midianites. When the angel of the Lord appeared to Gideon, he said, "The Lord is with you, mighty warrior."

"But sir," Gideon replied, "if the Lord is with us, why has all this happened to us? Where are all his wonders that our fathers told us about when they said, 'Did not the Lord bring us up out of Egypt?' But now the Lord has abandoned us and put us into the hand of Midian."

The Lord turned to him and said, "Go in the strength you have and save Israel out of Midian's hand. Am I not sending you?"

"But Lord," Gideon asked, "how can I save Israel? My clan is the weakest in Manasseh, and I am the least in my family."

The Lord answered, "I will be with you...."
— Judges 6:11-16 (NIV)

25

"You teach?"

The words roused me from my concentration. I stopped practicing the piano and looked at the man that had interrupted my work.

"Yes," I replied.

In reality, I had never taught. I wanted to teach, but had never had the opportunity to do so. I was sixteen years old and diligently working toward my goal of attending a conservatory after I graduated from high school. Four hours of practice were crammed into my daily schedule and that day was no exception. This was despite the fact that my parents had hired a crew of men to paint our living room. I concentrated on my Bach fugue as the painters worked, and it was one of them that posed the question.

"I have an eight-year-old daughter," he continued, "that I think might enjoy playing the piano. She has spina bifida and is paralyzed from the waist down. Would you be interested in teaching her?"

Several weeks later, I opened our front door and there stood a little girl with glasses and light brown hair. She had a big grin on her face, and she leaned against a walker.

"I'm Maris, and I'm here to learn to play the piano."

Over the next year or so, I saw Maris once a week for her lesson. She was a bright girl, enjoyable to be with, and easy to teach. Each week she would scoot up onto the bench, open up her book, and play her pieces with great earnestness. Inexperienced as I was, I was not the piano teacher that she deserved.

In fact, deep within my heart, I had doubts that she could learn to play. I thought about how sitting at the piano required use of leg muscles, with your legs bracing your body to bear your weight as you control your hands to shape the music. I had never tried to teach someone with special needs. I wasn't certain what was possible.

However, I wanted to teach, and she was there to be taught. Since there was no line of students outside my front door, I wanted to make this work. Despite my naïveté and ignorance, she learned. As I watched her learn, I marveled at her spirit and her attitude. Her brown eyes held a gleam in them whenever she was presented with a challenge. There was nothing in which she did not find a way to participate.

"When you play the piano, there are different joints in your hands and arms that you use." I explained at her first lesson. "The first joint that is important is the shoulder joint — you use that to move your entire arm."

I moved my arms in a circular motion to demonstrate. Maris copied.

"Exactly," I said, "just like arm exercises in gym class!"

Gym class! What was I thinking? I wanted to smack my forehead. *Of course she doesn't take gym class ... how could she?*

"Hey!" She replied, with her eyes glowing again. "How did you know that I did arm exercises in gym class?"

That was the little girl that God had brought into my life. If the challenge was there, she would conquer it, and revel in her victory.

One day, as I was finishing some work in the kitchen, she arrived for her lesson.

My mother had let her in the front door, and I could hear the clapping of her walker on the floor as she headed toward the piano. As I entered the room, I pondered how difficult it must be for her to quietly sneak about her business when her walker was so loud.

Then I smiled as I realized that this was one thing that this little girl would be more than able to work around. As bright as she was, Maris would have no problem finding ways to outsmart the adults in her world.

Then a new thought entered my mind.

Wouldn't it be great to have a daughter like Maris? It would be an entirely different kind of blessing to parent a little girl who is not held back by what life had thrown at her.

The thought passed, but my memories of Maris stayed with me long past the time she studied piano. Years later, while preparing for the birth of Justin, those memories comforted me....

The doctor's final diagnosis was far from conclusive. He called the defect a "mysterious bump," and proclaimed the rest of my unborn baby as "overall healthy." He was trying to be comforting, but the words that echoed over and over again in my mind were: *Something is wrong with my baby's brain.*

Five months into my pregnancy, I had gone to the hospital for a routine ultrasound. This was the second ultrasound, and, as there were many more ahead of us, we had decided that Rob would not take off work for this one. Alone, and expecting no problems, I watched the baby on the monitor.

"There is the head ... feet ... spine...." The technician told me. She chatted as she scanned, and I wondered what was taking so long.

"I can't seem to get the right angle on the head, so I'm going to get the doctor to double check." She left the room, and I lay on the table, telling myself that this was not going to be a problem.

The technician returned, this time with my doctor. He began to scan, frowning as he guided the device over the baby's head again and again.

"Well," he said after several minutes of scanning, "the baby looks very healthy. The heart, the lungs, the kidneys are all fine. The brain appears fine, as well. However, there's some type of bump on the back of his head."

"Bump?" I said, my mouth suddenly parched. "What kind of bump?"

"I can't tell you. I don't see a hole in his skull, and I can't detect anything in the bump. It could be anything from a fatty tumor to a portion of the brain protruding through the skull."

"How big is it?"

"Right now it is about the size of a quarter. However, since I don't know what it is I can't tell you if it will remain this size or if it will grow."

I sat there trying to compose myself. All I wanted to do, though, was run out of that room. I didn't want them to watch me cry. I didn't want this nice doctor to know how his words broke my heart. I took a deep breath and spoke again.

"What do I do next?"

"I think the next step should be genetic counseling and an amniocentesis. The amnio will help us determine if there is any brain fluid leaking out — which would indicate if the bump is an open lesion. If that all looks good, then I would recommend that we just wait it out and deliver the baby as planned. If not, then we're probably looking at a C-section."

Tears streamed down my face. I couldn't move. I couldn't talk. I couldn't even open my eyes. I felt a hand on my shoulder, and the doctor spoke once more.

"It'll be okay. Other than the bump, the baby looks very healthy."

With that, they left the room. I changed out of the hospital gown as quickly as I could and practically ran out of the hospital. I just wanted to be alone with my grief. Once in our van, my head hit the steering wheel, and I sobbed uncontrollably.

Brain fluid leaking out ... a bump ... his brain looks intact, but I'm not certain ... it could be brain material protruding through a hole in the skull....

The reality of the situation hit me like I had run into a brick wall. There was something wrong with my baby, and it was not just anything. There was something wrong with his *brain.* The implications were tremendous: mental handicaps, physical disabilities, and possibly even death.

When I thought that I could cry no longer, I began the drive home. However, I made it as far as the first pay phone.

"Rob," I cried into the receiver, "I...." The words wouldn't come.

"What? What happened? Is the baby okay?"

"No ... I just finished the ultrasound. There is something ..." breathing deeply, I continued, "wrong with his head."

"Stay where you are, I'll be right there."

Within minutes, Rob had joined me in the parking lot of a convenience store outside the hospital. We both sat in the van and cried as we grieved the future we had planned for our child.

What do you do when you know that the child you are carrying has a birth defect? How do you face the ensuing months of pregnancy? I awoke the next morning, unsure of what to think or how to feel. I had four months of this pregnancy left, and I was certain that I could not spend the entire time crying.

I tried to pray, but I was too angry and too scared. The picture I had held in my mind of a beautiful, healthy baby was now gone. There was a loss there and with it came all the grief that accompanied that loss. That grief was coupled with great uncertainty — we did not know what the future held.

Emotionally drained by it all, I could hardly piece together the words to pray. So I laid before God what was on my heart.

I prayed, *Although I can't pray without ceasing, the cry of my heart is for my baby.*

The apostle Paul wrote that "the Spirit intercedes for us with groans that words cannot express" (NIV), and over the next few months I relied on him to do that for me. To even verbalize my fears and the pain that they brought was more than I could do. All I could bring before God were two words, "my baby."

For the next four months, those two words were the cry of my heart. They were the cry of my soul, my body, and my mind. Every fiber of my being cried out to God on behalf of my child, every moment of every day, even though I felt as though my lips could not form the words. I am confident that the Holy Spirit took that cry to God, and he gave those words the meaning that they needed. God searched my heart and mind, never requiring me to be eloquent with my words. He heard that cry, understood what it meant, and acted upon it.

Although not constant, I began to feel a peace in the midst of all the strife. The peace came at the times when I could focus my thoughts on the sovereignty of God, trusting that he was in control. A battle raged in my mind; thoughts that focused on leaking brain fluid, brain damage, and infant mortality, and thoughts that focused on God's sovereignty and control. The situation did not change, but the more I meditated on God's control, the stronger his peace became in me. As time moved on, I became more capable of trusting him. The more I trusted him, the more his peace was in me.

Along the way, we were given encouragement even beyond his peace. Weekly visits to the doctor, coupled with ultrasounds, showed that, although the bump was still there, the baby was growing and developing as expected. Also, the amnio showed no leakage of brain fluid, and it revealed that the baby was a boy.

"I want to name him Justin," I told Rob, after we had heard the news.

"What does it mean?" he asked.

"Justice — one who brings justice."

So, on that day, the baby became Justin. He became a person, a treasure, one that we hoped would grow up and help bring justice to people who are oppressed. He was a gift from God, not only to us, but to all his life would touch.

The package that a gift comes in has no connection to the value of the gift, and it is no different when that gift is a child. God had begun to give us a picture of who Justin would be, and we were ready to gladly accept that gift regardless of if it was packaged in a body or mind that did not look like we had first expected.

Justin continued to grow, and all the prenatal tests indicated that he was healthy and strong. My prayers continued to grow stronger, bolder, and braver.

"What do you think of the name Nicholas?" I asked Rob.

"I like that — for the middle name?"

"Yes, and do you know what it means?" I asked.

"No, what?"

"Triumphant."

The day finally arrived when Justin Nicholas would make his debut. His delivery progressed without a glitch, and soon I was holding my nine-pound baby boy. I looked at his head and tried not to allow my fears to overwhelm the joy of seeing this beautiful gift for the first time.

Exhausted as I was from over an hour of pushing, I forced myself to examine the bump on his head. It was large, much bigger than we had expected, and it was slightly bruised.

Funny, I thought, *I could've sworn the bump was supposed to be on the back of his head, not his forehead. And, it's so huge — it is more the size of a bullfrog than a quarter....*

Rob took him in his arms while the doctors finished up with me. I watched as he studied Justin's forehead, and I saw the fear that he was trying to hide in his eyes. The lump was big, and, it had obviously grown. Rob flipped Justin over to pat his back. A smile spread across his face.

"Deb! Look!" he said, showing me the back of Justin's head. "This is the bump!"

Sure enough, there was a quarter-sized mysterious bump on the back of Justin's head. "That wasn't the bump on his forehead — that's just the shape of his head!"

We laughed at the mix up, and thanked God for Justin's large head, misshapen by a rough trip down the birth canal.

Soon, a pediatric neurologist arrived, and Justin was taken from us and placed in the Neonatal Intensive Care Unit. I was moved to a recovery room, all the while asking for my baby. My nurse in recovery was not sympathetic.

"You may visit the baby in NICU when you can walk."

Walk! I had had an epidural! I had no idea how long it would take me to walk, and I needed to nurse him. Only an hour had passed since I had delivered, and I could barely feel my legs. The nurse told me that I could prove to her my ability to walk to NICU by first taking myself to the bathroom.

Twenty minutes after she left, I called her back.

"I am ready to walk to the bathroom."

"No. There's no way. The epidural is still too strong. Can you even feel your legs?"

"Yes," I lied. I wanted to be with my baby.

I made it exactly one step before I fell back on the bed.

"You'll have to wait," she said, and she left the room. Poking her head back in, she pulled the divider curtain closed. "By the way, you're getting a roommate."

I laid in the bed and cried. Rob had gone home to be with Ben, and, once again, I was alone. My arms ached to hold my baby, and I was angry that I had been put in this position. As I wallowed in my anger, I listened through the curtain as the nurses prepared the room for my roommate.

"This is number four for this mom."

"Is she nursing?"

"No, and she'll keep the baby in the nursery unless she wants a visit."

"I put the formula over here by the bassinet, just in case she decides to keep the baby with her."

"Sounds good, but I doubt it will matter. She wants the baby in the nursery."

That was it. I had had enough. After all that we had been through, this was the last straw.

Here I am, I raged at God, *living in the faith that you will care for us. I'm trusting that you'll do what is best. I've given my life over to caring for these two.... I am a good parent. How could you do this to us? Why do I have the sick baby and SHE, the one who doesn't even want the child with her, gets the healthy baby? Why us?*

I didn't care about blasphemy; I didn't care about eternal damnation. I wanted answers. From my perspective, it just wasn't fair that God had allowed this to happen. I had tried to be faithful and obedient. I had done my best to be a good parent, and I just couldn't understand how he could do this to us or to Justin.

Then, I clearly heard God's first direct words about this situation: "It's because you are good parents that I have allowed this. It is you I have trusted with this."

I tried to understand, but it still didn't make sense. I wanted a healthy baby. How could an unhealthy baby be something God would give as a gift? But as I thought about those words, I began to see God's perspective. This mysterious growth on his head was a burden. However, Justin wasn't. He was a gift, and this bump was an obstacle that God, in his infinite wisdom, entrusted us with which to be faithful. It was an honor that God entrusted to us. We had been specially chosen to be his parents, for an unknown task that lay ahead. It was then that I gained the courage and strength I needed to move on. I pushed the nurse's call button again. Within minutes she was in the room.

"I need to use the bathroom." I declared (in reality, I needed to nurse my baby, but that was the direct route to getting there).

With that, I slung my legs out of the bed, and holding on for dear life, began the treacherous walk to the bathroom. Five minutes later, with strict warnings from the nurse not to lock the door, I was standing near the toilet, holding onto the counter. I quietly waited a few seconds, flushed, washed my hands and stumbled back out the door. I avoided eye contact in the hope that I had tricked her into believing that I had actually used the restroom.

I settled back in the bed and looked at the nurse.

"I want to go see my baby." I had no idea how I was going to walk down the hall all the way to the NICU, but I was certain that nothing was going to stop me.

"Good. I'll go get you a wheelchair."

"A wheelchair? I thought I had to be able to walk."

"Well, now that I know you're strong enough I know that you won't cause any problems for the NICU nurses. So, I'll wheel you down."

Several weeks later, I kissed Justin on the forehead and handed him over to the neurosurgeon for brain surgery. The mysterious bump had been diagnosed: a cranial menegecil. It was the rarest of all neural tube defects, and also the most benign. A very small portion of his skull had developed around a ventricle in his brain, allowing it to protrude through his skull and form an "extra chamber" between the skull and skin. Everything else was exactly as it should be, so this defect was completely correctable with one surgery.

At one month of age, Justin underwent three hours of brain surgery. That afternoon, for the first time, he lifted his head to look at the world around him. A week later, he smiled for the first time. By the time he was two months old he was laughing out loud. Over the next few years, he grew into a little boy who loved dirt, bugs, books, and dinosaurs. That terrible time of grief and fear was hardly ever thought of again, for Justin had absolutely no lasting problems from his birth defect. Justin was triumphant.

As Justin grew and healed, I knew that we had seen the hand of God at work. Not so much in his life, but in ours. We were changed. God had revealed to us a new depth of understanding about the inherent value of a life. As parents, we had faced a rocky road with our child and had come out victorious and emboldened. Each milestone that Justin reached had additional value, as we pondered what had gone on before. It reminded me of the pride that came about from Maris' successes with the piano.

At the time I prayed that simple prayer about God granting us a girl, I believe he knew that all the pieces for his plan were falling into place. As I began to research adoption, domestic and international, I found a recurring need: the need for families to adopt waiting children — children that are often passed over for adoption because of their age or a special need. I learned that when these waiting children were not adopted, no matter what country they were in, they faced a future so bleak that most American's could not even begin to fathom it. In all the adoption literature I received, there was one country that consistently popped up as being in desperate need for adoptive families for handicapped children: Ukraine.

When I prayed, I would think about my experiences with Maris, and, of course, our experiences with Justin. I wanted to see God take our experience with Justin and make it into something beautiful. I wanted God's lessons to produce fruit that fed not only us, but other people, as well. After all, Justin was to be a person who brought justice. I began to see special-needs adoption as a way God could use our experience as a means to carry his peace to another person.

The thought was intimidating. We had prepared ourselves for special needs with Justin, as we had no choice. But to intentionally take on a child with a disability sounded insane. To travel across the world to Ukraine and adopt a special-needs child was a task that neither Rob nor I believed we could accomplish. But God would not back down, and when I challenged him, he replied with the story of Gideon.

As the story begins, God finds Gideon quietly threshing wheat in a winepress. His unique way of completing his task is not due to creativity, but the fact that he is trying to hide from the Midianites (the people who had conquered Israel). The occupation of Israel by the Midianites had been so terrible that they "did not spare a living thing for Israel" (NIV). The Israelites cried out to God for help, and he chose quiet, insecure Gideon to accomplish the task.

When God presented him with the task of driving out the Midianites, Gideon did not exactly jump at the opportunity. Instead, he questioned God's choice.

"But Lord," Gideon asked, "how can I save Israel? My clan is the weakest ... and I am the least in my family."

I instantly saw the parallel with our family.

"But Lord, how can I adopt a special-needs child from Ukraine? We have no money, no connections in Ukraine, and we're clueless about international travel."

God's answer to Gideon was his answer to me.

"I will be with you," answered the Lord.

There was no possibility that Gideon could, even in the best circumstances, win this battle. However, God never intended him to do so. As the story unfolds, God calls Gideon to even greater faith when he slashes the size of the Israelite army down to 300 men. In the end, those 300 men defeated an army estimated to be well over 100,000 strong.

It was the same with this adoption. There was no way that we could accomplish the task in front of us. The battle would be far beyond what we could win. However, God did not expect us to go it alone. "I will be with you," answered the Lord.

Even so, Gideon did not just take God at his word. Before agreeing to follow God, Gideon asked him for some very specific signs. He laid a fleece out in the grass before retiring to bed. He asked God to soak the fleece in dew, but to keep the ground dry.

The next morning the fleece was wet enough for him to wring it out.

Still not convinced, he once again laid a fleece out before he went to bed. This time he asked God to soak the ground with dew, but leave the fleece dry.

The next morning the fleece was dry and the ground wet. He was convinced. In the spirit of Gideon we asked for some signs, and the fleeces that we laid out were very specific.

The first request I raised to him was to bring someone into our lives who had been to Ukraine. How I could ever have forgotten that our church had numerous ties to that country is beyond me. But, on that day, I needed to know that if we brought a child home from Ukraine there would be some tangible way for us to connect her with her birth country. The request was simple: Show me someone who had traveled to Ukraine.

Later that day, I ran out to the pharmacy to pick up a prescription. The line was unusually long, and as I stood there waiting, I realized that there was someone else in line I knew. I stepped back in line so that we could chat while we waited.

"This is some line," I said.

"Yes," she replied. "But, I never complain about lines anymore. Not ever since my trip to Ukraine. The lines there are worse than anything anyone here could imagine."

I was so surprised, I had a difficult time responding.

"You've ... been ... to ... Ukraine?" I asked. "What did you do there?"

"Well, I went on one of the mission trips there with the church. You know, there are a lot of people from church who have been to Ukraine." (Okay, so God did not answer with just one person, but with a multitude....)

"I think that God is calling us to adopt a child from there," I blurted out.

"The orphanages are full, and the children are so beautiful. Almost all of them have special needs."

My mind was alive with questions as I raced home. I told Rob what had happened. He got out the atlas and began looking for "*the* Ukraine" (we had much to learn). We decided to pray some more and threw out another fleece.

"Okay, we know people who have been to Ukraine. But what about people *from* Ukraine? How can I keep her connected to her country of origin if she knows no one from there?"

That one was answered even faster. Several minutes later, the phone rang. It was a friend of mine who happened to work at a nonprofit agency who hosted international guests to our city. We chatted for a couple minutes and she asked me about the adoption plans.

"We're considering Ukraine."

37

"Ukraine! That's great! I have a friend who immigrated from there. He works as a translator for us sometimes!"

God was now two for two. Still, we were not ready to commit. However, for the next several days, Ukraine was constantly on my mind, and, in small ways, God continued to send his messages.

The next morning I read a newspaper article about our sister city: Kharkov, Ukraine. Later that week, two of my piano students brought in music that they wanted to learn: The Ukrainian Christmas song, "Carol Of The Bells." And, each night I found myself scanning the pictures of the children on Ukrainian adoption websites, wondering what our daughter would look like.

Soon after that, we were certain. God was calling us to adopt a child from Ukraine. We just had to figure out how.

The Battle Plan

If we fight the Lord's battles merely by duplicating the way the world does its work, we are like little boys playing with wooden swords pretending they are in the battle while their big brothers are away in some distant bloody land.

— Francis Schaeffer, *Death in the City* (Downers Grove, Illinois: InterVarsity Press, 1969), p. 142

This is no afternoon athletic contest that we'll walk away from and forget about in a couple of hours. This is for keeps, a life-or-death fight to the finish against the devil and all his angels.

— Ephesians 6:12 (The Message)

The remnant of Israel will do no wrong; they will speak no lies, nor will deceit be found in their mouths. They will eat and lie down and no one will make them afraid.

— Zephaniah 3:13 (NIV)

It was a race to beat the clock at the Ukrainian Embassy in Chicago. All of our documents were compiled and ready to be sent to Ukraine for translation. However, before their transatlantic flight they had to have a series of bureaucratic stamps placed on them, the most expensive of which came from the Ukrainian Embassy. At that time, the embassy in Chicago offered a service called "bundling," where they would take related documents and "bundle" them together requiring only one authentication stamp for several documents rather than one per document. The bundling saved hundreds of dollars — in our case it was the difference between about $400 and $1,600.

Unfortunately, as I was finishing up the dossier, the Chicago embassy issued a warning that sometime in the next few weeks they were going to suspend the practice of bundling documents. Until that time, I was dragging my feet with the paperwork, as we didn't have money to move forward. But, upon hearing the news, I changed gears and finished as quickly as possible. There was still one small problem though....

We did not have the $400 necessary to cover the embassy fee. Time was ticking away, bringing us closer to the time when bundling would no longer be an option, and the bill would increase by $1,200. I finished the paperwork on a Thursday afternoon, but it sat, untouched, on my desk until Sunday. That morning, someone at church walked up to me and gave me a check for $400.

The following Monday, I began the race. Before the paperwork could be shipped to Chicago, it had to be verified by our county, state, and federal governments (traveling through Cincinnati, Columbus, and Washington DC). As I drove downtown to have our notaries verified, I realized the value of the documents that I was carrying. The months of work attributed a certain amount of value (none of the documents were easily replaced), but what those documents represented had an eternal value to them. They were compiled to save the life of a child.

For the first time, I became aware of the battle into which our family had jumped.

As I drove downtown for the county's stamp of approval, nagging doubts entered my mind. They started small.

There are never any parking spaces downtown. It'll take hours just to find one. Better plan to take the papers to Columbus on a different day.

I drove on, arrived downtown, and did find a parking spot. However, I had been directed to find the wrong building. Led by a well-meaning secretary who happened to answer the phone, I had driven to the Justice Center. After searching for about thirty minutes for the notary commission room, I stopped and asked a clerk for help.

"I need to find the department that certifies notary commissions for adoptions."

"All adoption related stuff is through the Department of Human Services," he replied with a grin. Then he turned to his co-worker and said, "Am I good or what? I know it all!"

"But," I interrupted, "this isn't for a county adoption, but an international one. I need to have my notaries verified...."

"Doesn't matter," he smiled at me, so smug about his knowledge. "If it's adoption related it is Department of Human Services." Then he shut his window.

Frustrated, I left the building and started on the walk to the Department of Human Services. Instinctively knowing that his advice must be incorrect, I stopped right where I was and used my cell phone to call Rob at work.

"Hold on," he said, "let me check online." He returned a minute later. "You need to go to the third floor of the courthouse for notary commissions."

Already livid that I had spent nearly half an hour walking out of my way because of some government worker's arrogant attitude, my anger was heightened by the fact that I was standing right outside of the court house. The building was directly across the street from the Justice Center. As I walked, thoughts continued to simply pop into my mind.

So much time wasted, you should just give up for today ... really this is more than you can do right now. You have an excuse ... you were lost and misdirected. Go home, rest until tomorrow. There's no rule that says this has to be done today.

I finally arrived at the notary commission. As he checked each paper, he verified the notary. All was fine — except for one. Although the notary had told me that she was certified for our county, she was actually certified by the county to our north. Her stamp simply could not be verified by our courthouse.

For some reason, beyond what I could understand, it was more than I could handle. I was shameless. I started to cry.

"Look," the short, crusty, old notary officer told me, "just get a different notary to sign it. As long as there's a county certified notary on it, I can put the certification stamp there."

"Okay." I replied, knowing that I was overreacting. "It's been a long day."

"There is a bank just across the street, you know. You could ask there...." He was trying to be helpful.

I gathered up all my papers and raced out the door and across the street to the bank. However, there was not a notary there that was willing to verify a signature at the request of a person they did not know. I left the bank in tears.

Give it up! The voice repeated. This time it was louder, and it was starting to sound less like me thinking and more like someone suggesting something ... *you're not going to get through all this today. Just go home.*

I didn't go home, but I did go back to the car. I sat there, trying to decide what to do next. I called Rob again and asked him for directions to the other courthouse. The line was silent while he was looking. I had already started driving when he came back.

"I got the directions," he said, "but there is something that you need to know. I looked the notary up in their database and she's not there. On a hunch I looked under past years. She was there, only her commission has now expired. She's not a valid notary."

See, my mind was raging, *there is no way out of this mess. Just throw in the towel.*

"What can I do?" I asked Rob. It was a rhetorical question, as I thought he would not have the answer. To my surprise, he did.

We had a friend who had done some of the notary work for us earlier on. He suggested I call her at work. I did, and she was in her office that was just off the exit I was approaching on the highway.

Within fifteen minutes, I was headed back downtown with my paper notarized. I found a spot, parked, ran up to the notary commissioner, and had my paper certified. It was a great victory!

Until ... I looked at the time back in the car. It was early afternoon, and I had to drive two hours to Columbus in order to get the papers state certified.

Too much, the voice said, *too much for one day....*

But I just moved on. I was so tired and as I drove further and further away from home, a sense of fear came over me. The cars on either side seemed to dart like arrows all around me. It felt like they were trying to hit me.

I'm getting paranoid, I thought.

However, the fear increased. My spine started to tingle, and it felt like someone was sitting behind me, leering at my every effort. I was distracted and agitated.

I can't drive ... I am going to get lost in Columbus ... How will I get back to the highway ... I can't navigate Columbus, how will I ever navigate Ukraine? ... I am all alone ... there is no one I know here who could help me if I needed it ... it will be worse in Ukraine ... I can't do this ... I am all alone, if anything goes wrong there is no one here to help me....

The thoughts climaxed until the fear that filled my car almost seemed to take a form, and I felt as though I could feel the very breath of Satan on my neck. It was then that I recognized my enemy.

Get behind me, Satan ... I can do all things through Christ Jesus who saves me!

For the remainder of the day, I meditated on that thought. *I can do all things through Christ Jesus who saves me.*

I chanted it as I drove. I prayed it when I was lost in Columbus, and I said it as I pulled back into my driveway with the paperwork completed.

The next morning, I sent our dossier, certification stamps, and all, to the federal government and forwarded them from there to the Ukrainian Embassy. The paperwork was now out of my hands. It had taken six months to get this far.

Our journey began with a long wait. We knew what God was calling us to do, and, almost instantly, we found options for how to pursue it. The problem was that there were so many options, but there seemed to be no direct leading from God. Within weeks we had found a local social service agency that was willing to provide the home study. We were even able to begin the process ... but we could only get so far without knowing who would help us in Ukraine. This lack of direction led to many late nights at my computer searching the internet for answers. It was one of those nights that God began to reveal his plan.

I rubbed my eyes and looked at the computer screen again. I could not believe what I was reading.

"Why spend thousands of dollars on an agency?"

This really sounded too good to be true. For months, I had been researching adoption agencies, certain that we would have to choose one to complete this adoption. After writing letters and calling over twenty international agencies, I was very discouraged. It seemed like every agency differed on so many issues — the adoption process, criteria for adoptive parents, and available children. Yet, they were all similar in one way: The estimated cost of an adoption was always $25,000 to $35,000, and they all warned of the dangers of trying to "go it alone" (without the use of an agency) for your international adoption.

This website was contradicting all of that by showing photos of over 400 children successfully, and legally, adopted from Ukraine without the use of an agency.

In disbelief, I decided to verify this by comparing it to the information that was posted on the US State Department's website. This website is designed to educate Americans on the legal adoption process in every country that allows international adoption. And, it did, indeed, verify everything. The adoption system in Ukraine was designed to be accessible to any person interested in adopting from Ukraine.

Most countries send a prospective adoptive parent what is called a referral (a picture and information on a child that they have selected for the parent). Ukraine, however, simply approves the parents to adopt. The parents then fly to Kyiv, where they meet with the director of what was then called the National Adoption Center. She interviews them, places her stamp of approval on the adoption, and then sends them down the hall to the psychologist. The psychologist then interviews the couple and allows them to look through the information on all the available children.

Although we read that the estimates of the number of orphaned children in Ukraine ranged from 20,000 to 100,000, we were never certain what the exact number was. However, photos and brief medical histories of each of those children are kept in binders in the psychologist's office in Kyiv. There are 25 *oblasts*, or regions, in Ukraine, and there is a binder full of children for each region, with additional binders assigned to the largest cities.

The parents peruse the binders of information, and then choose a child to visit. Upon meeting the child, they can then decide if they want to adopt that child or meet a different one. Once they have met a child they want to adopt, they set a court date, and complete the adoption.

Even though I was an American citizen, I had access to that public system. By avoiding an agency, we would save over $10,000 on the adoption. All we had to do was find an honest Ukrainian to serve as our translator and provide us with the list of necessary paperwork.

While I was overjoyed at the savings, I had to admit to myself one thing. *The entire thing was crazy! An independent adoption from Ukraine?*

I would like to believe that I continued considering this option because I wanted to grow my faith in new ways. I would like to believe that I desired a real adventure, trusting only God to pave the way for us to Ukraine. Ironically, it was my lack of faith that God would really provide the money that led me to continue down this path. I wanted to save $10,000 to $15,000.

I prayerfully held onto the hope that we could find that honest Ukrainian. As I prayed, I diligently looked.

Ukraine was a popular country to adopt from, and I easily located many independent lawyers and translators who could help us with the adoption. There had been a desire in my heart, from the very start of the adoption, to find a righteous person in Ukraine to help us. We had heard the stories and read the newspaper articles. We understood. Corruption was rampant in Ukraine. However, we believed that there was a remnant of believers and that God was still at work there.

We wanted our daughter to know that God loved Ukraine, and that despite the years of persecution, his love flourished and changed people there. We wanted to be able to show her pictures of the people who loved her enough to help her find hope, not because they were paid to, but because they understood the inherent value of her life.

This is not to say that people who are paid to facilitate adoptions care only for the profit and not about the future of the children. However, there was more that we were looking for. We wanted another miracle.

The problem was, though, that I was impatient. I was not willing to wait for God to bring about that miracle. I wanted to move on, so I did. I had a nagging fear that if I didn't make things happen, nothing would happen. At the base of this fear was one that nagged at the back of my mind through the entire adoption.

What if we failed? What were the implications? Did that mean, then, that God did not exist? Did that mean that what I had heard had not been the voice of God but the voice of my own desire? Would no answer come because there was no one there to orchestrate the events? I had faith, but then there were times when I did not. My mind was a battleground between faith and doubt.

The gospel of Mark includes a story about a father who reflects the struggle I was facing. His son was possessed by an evil spirit. When it presented itself, the boy would throw himself on the ground, convulsing and foaming at the mouth. It was terrifying and dangerous, and the boy's father knew that if anyone could heal his son, it was Jesus. But even then, when the father had seen so much physical evidence of spiritual battles, there was an "if"....

> *"It has often thrown him into fire or water to kill him. But if you can do anything, take pity on us and help us."*

46

"If you can?" said Jesus. "Everything is possible for him who believes." Immediately the boy's father exclaimed, "I do believe; help me overcome my unbelief!" — Mark 9: 22-23 (NIV)

Belief and unbelief — they both resided in my heart, and when the adoption process started, it was often my unbelief that led the way. But, God, in his mercy, would step in and save me, and so it was with finding a translator.

Wanting to get to Ukraine and bring home my daughter, I decided to move ahead. I spent hours researching adoption programs, filling out applications, and checking people's references. I went so far as to officially apply to one particular program simply to get the ball rolling. All along the way, though, none of them felt right. If I had simply waited, God did plan to fill the need.

One night, I decided to take a break from all my adoption work and went to a party at a friend's house. As a group of ladies sat around, chatting and playing board games, I began a conversation with a person I had never met before.

"We are trying to adopt a child," I told her as we talked about our families. "We think God is leading us to Ukraine, but we aren't getting very far."

"Really? I have some friends who just returned from Ukraine with a child. I could pass your phone number on to them, and I'm sure they could give you some advice."

I gave her our phone number, doubtful that her friends would have the time to call us. Despite my doubts, several days later I got a phone call from that family. They had just returned home from Ukraine and they had adopted a little boy.

As we discussed their time in Ukraine, she mentioned that they had used a well-known independent adoption facilitator. Although the adoption was successful, she had one regret. There was a church in Kyiv that had just started an adoption facilitation program and she wished that it had been up and running for them. The church was called Calvary Chapel.

"If I was to do this again," she said, "I would much rather use Calvary Chapel."

I jumped online and found their website. Calvary Chapel Kyiv was a growing church, planted by American missionaries. Sure enough, among their many outreaches, they had just started an adoption facilitation ministry. The church saw adoption into a loving Christian family as a means to evangelize.

Immediately, I emailed them (their address was actually adoptinukraine@aol.com!). Within days I received a reply from Ira, a lovely young woman who served as a translator for Calvary Chapel Kyiv, who would, ultimately, be the facilitator of our adoption. She gave instructions on how to proceed with collecting the paperwork. Once all the paperwork was ready, we simply needed to forward it, with a small translation fee, to Kyiv. The remaining money (a fraction of the cost of other translators or agencies) was paid when we arrived in Ukraine. This was a ministry of the church, so no single person was directly profiting from the adoption.

The next few months were spent preparing the paperwork, arranging travel plans, child care, and gathering the money to pay for it all. Emails back and forth between here and Ukraine, along with the free consultation of an American lawyer who was helping with the ministry, prepared us for the road that lay ahead.

Throughout all the preparations, I was often amazed by one fact. Despite all the odds stacked against us, God had provided exactly who we were looking for to help us complete the adoption. That fact gave us the courage to be bolder in our prayers and braver in our dreams. We defined who we wanted to adopt: a girl, age three or younger, with physical special needs, and in faith we named her Anna.

Our work continued until our last battle on this side of the ocean: document authentication. Once I named the enemy, won the battle, and shipped the documents, we had nothing left to do but wait — wait and pray.

A Word About Money

It is an unfortunate human failing that a full pocket-book often groans more loudly than an empty stomach.
— Franklin Delano Roosevelt

I am opposed to millionaires, but it would be dangerous to offer me the position. — Mark Twain

Whoever loves money never has money enough; whoever loves wealth is never satisfied with his income. This too is meaningless. — Ecclesiastes 5:10 (NIV)

No one can serve two masters. Either he will hate the one and love the other, or he will be devoted to the one and despise the other. You cannot serve both God and Money. — Matthew 6:24 (NIV)

Adoption is expensive and there is no way around it. It costs thousands of dollars to pay for home studies, agency fees, airplane tickets, accommodations in foreign countries, translators, and governmental fees. Even the fees to become a US citizen total nearly $1,000.

The cost to adopt scared me and it did so for one reason: We did not have the money to cover all the expenses. Our money situation was the most tangible and obvious obstacle in this adoption. Other areas we could accomplish on our own strength. We could wow social workers, submit to background checks, and pull together all the paperwork. But, we could not produce money where there was none. This opened up the possibility of two different endings to our adoption story. Scenario number one was that God would not provide and that we would not complete the adoption. In my thoughts, the meaning behind that was that it implied that we were completely crazy and had never heard God speak because he did not exist (and, therefore, *could not* provide for us) or, because he does exist but never spoke to us. Neither was an inspiring option.

Of course, those doubts were based on a train of thought that followed the "health, wealth, and prosperity" theology that, although I would never profess to believe, often manages to weave its way into my thinking. At the back of my mind constantly lurks the thought that God would call us to something, only if that something is successful ... never mind about martyrs, the persecuted church, or any other suffering Christian in the world. Those doubts also did not allow for the fact that God could call us to do this adoption for some other purpose than the adoption itself. As we moved along, ever aware that the entire thing could fall through at any moment, I had to accept that the outcome was not my responsibility. I was only responsible to follow God to the next step in the process. However, I struggled in my faith to keep the right perspective on just what defined success, and money loomed over me as a large part of that definition.

As each prayer was answered, we moved one step closer to the end, and that left me with a different problem: the second scenario. In that scenario, God would provide and we would adopt our little girl. Though it was what we wanted, it, too, raised two very pertinent questions. How would God provide? What did we need to do in order to find God's provision?

50

Most people who have been Christians for any length of time have heard stories of someone walking up to a person and giving them a check for the exact amount of money they needed at that moment. Sometimes it is cash from an anonymous source or a reimbursement check that arrived in the mail ... some kind of story where "boom" the money was there.

We really wanted a story like that: a rich, unknown uncle dies and leaves us $25,000 or a person so moved by God to help us just drops a check for $10,000 off at our house. It would have been so easy that way! However, the easy path is hardly ever the path God leads us down. What will we learn along the way if it is all so simple?

The first step we took was to spend our savings on our home study fee and INS (Immigration and Naturalization Services) fees. Then, with a pitiful amount left for emergencies, we waited on God. After a month or so of waiting for that spectacular amount of money to fall down from heaven, we decided that God was waiting on us for something. So, we cut back in every area that was possible (which was not that many areas) and I took on some extra odd jobs and piano students.

It was quickly apparent that our income was not going to provide enough money. We found a ministry that aided adoptive families by collecting the money donated to their adoptions and providing tax receipts for those donations. We applied and were accepted into their ministry. We then began to raise funds by sending out letters explaining about the adoption. Before long, people who wanted to be a part of what God was doing began to donate. But, as time moved on, we could see that it was not going to be enough.

We were at a real crossroads. So much evangelical teaching has berated debt, and yet, a loan was the only option that was presenting itself. Time was marching on, we were still several thousand dollars short of our goal, and I was a person very confused about how much we should do and how much God should do.

If I really had faith, I scolded myself, *I would continue to move forward never considering a loan an option. My faith is weak....*

Not having the money in hand nagged at me and thoughts of failure buzzed around my mind like an annoying fly.

Where is your provision, God? I demanded.

I wanted it to be perfect. By that, I mean that I wanted it to look good and debt did not look good. Taking on debt, in my mind, made it look like we had never really heard God but that we were making this adoption happen on our own initiative. But, as the time for travel approached, I felt as though we had no choice.

"I think we need to take out a home equity line of credit, just in case we need it," I said one day.

"I agree," Rob replied.

You're both a couple of faithless wimps, Satan whispered in my mind.

It was then I realized that God was calling us to even greater faith. This was not a loan for a boat, an expensive car, or a larger house. It was a loan to save the life of a child. God had spoken to many people who generously helped us. And, I believe, he spoke to many more who never took that step of faith. God will provide for his work through his church, but he will never force anyone to obey. He invited others, but they chose not to be a part of it. He made another way ... one that would resolve itself in its own time. We opened our line of credit for this adoption knowing that we were not being faithless fools. God would provide and he did.

Over three years later, while at a picnic, a large dog ran across the yard without warning or provocation, jumped up into my face, and bit my nose and lip. It continued to attack me, but the majority of damage had been done. The result of the fifteen-second attack was enormous: over fifty stitches in my face and a mind that was shaken to the point of terror.

I was rushed to the hospital where God began to put the pieces back together. The hospital chaplain came in to pray for me. After he prayed, he sat with me.

"God can redeem this," I said, heavily sedated, yet still in shock.

"Yes, he can," he replied. "He didn't do this to you, but he can use it."

"He can make this into something beautiful...." My words were slurred from both the drugs and my torn lips.

"He can make anything beautiful," replied the chaplain.

The plastic surgeon on call happened to be one of the best in the country and he intricately pieced my face back together. Later that afternoon I was home, stitched up, but still terrified.

Months of healing followed and the distress of Post-Traumatic Stress Disorder filled our home. Constantly jumpy and nervous, I was unable to handle it when the children were loud (especially when they would, while being silly, jump out at me and yell, "Boo!"), a sudden noise happened, or a dog came near our yard. My sleep was tormented with violent nightmares. Walks in the park, even around our neighborhood, became filled with moments of terror when I would see a dog.

Through it all, though, God worked. My face healed faster and better than the surgeon predicted. My heart and mind healed, too, although it took much longer than the physical wounds. I will always have scarring above my lip and on my nose, but that scarring is now a reminder of how God healed me and then made the ordeal beautiful.

In the end, I was entitled to money for my pain and suffering. Money enough to pay off the adoption debt *and* to help several other families bring home waiting children. What was intended for evil, God used for good.

The beautiful end to the story was not one that I knew when we made the decision for the loan. That decision was made in faith that God would always provide. He had called us to take on the debt, and, ultimately, it is he who controls the systems of the world in which we live — to use for his purposes. I learned that we need to listen to the voice of God and not confuse that with the opinions of those who are outspoken in the church.

The process of God providing was just that, a process. There were moments when we did receive large gifts — hundreds of dollars or airplane tickets. But most often, he provided what we needed for the next leg of the marathon, and not the entire race.

Since our adoption, many people have told me that they, too, are interested in adopting.

"I would love to adopt ... but we just don't have the money."

While there are many good reasons a person might have for not adopting a child, money is not one of them. Money should never be a reason that a person of faith decides not to follow a path of righteousness. No matter how valuable your home, your car, or your annual vacation, nothing is as valuable as the life of that child you might have adopted. Nothing.

Atheists And Customs Agents

One day, a rich Russian asked a friend for his opinion on where to take a vacation.

"An African safari might be a good idea," the friend replied.

"What exactly do you do on a safari?"

"You get to buy a new wardrobe and jeep, and then you drive around, looking out the windows and shooting."

"No, that won't work, it doesn't sound relaxing ... it sounds like my job."

— A popular joke about the Russian New Rich

I am sending you out like sheep among wolves. There-fore be as shrewd as snakes and as innocent as doves.
— Matthew 10:16 (NIV)

The winter snow turned to slush, and, for a time, a gray dreari-ness settled over our home. The boys played inside with all of their energy filling every nook and cranny, until it seemed like our house was going to explode. They chased each other, pretending one was Peter and the other was the wolf. They drew pictures, read books, and hunted for insects that might have made the mistake of finding their way into our home.

They were completely unaware of how they broke my heart.

I would watch them play and, at times my heart would weep at the thought of leaving them. It seemed so wrong. I had been with the boys since their births, and now, while they were still so young, I was ready to leave them for an undetermined amount of time — all to adopt a child whom I did not even know. The problem of raising enough money paled in comparison to the problem of leaving my boys.

Throughout the adoption, the thought of leaving the boys would wander into my mind. If things went well in Ukraine, then we could possibly be in and out in less than three weeks. However, if things went poorly, then we could be caught up in the adoption for months, unsure of when we could go home.

As those thoughts nagged me, I would push them out of my mind, concentrating, instead, on whatever task was at hand. I continually told myself the same thing: *I will deal with the pain of leaving them when that time comes.*

The problem was, though, that that time was fast approaching. And, one spring morning I found myself packing our suitcases while the boys sat on the floor next to me and looked at books.

"Are the cheerios for Anna?" Justin asked.

No matter how unreal their sister felt to me, Anna was a real person to Ben and Justin. They prayed for her daily, drew pictures for her, and dreamed about the day that she would finally be home.

"Yes," I said, "or they might be for me or Daddy, if we want a bowl of cereal."

"Don't they have cereal in Ukraine?"

"Well, I am sure that they do, but we need to have a lot stuff with us in case we aren't able to get to a store."

The problem with planning for this trip was that we had no idea where we were going, who we were going to adopt, when she would start to stay with us — anything. We had been advised by others who had made the trip to assemble a large collection of items such as toilet paper, flashlights, dried food, and duct tape in addition to the regular international travel items. It felt as though I was packing for an international camping trip, except for the cash. All our expenses would be paid in cash, and we had been advised, time and again, that credit cards and traveler's checks were worthless in Ukraine. We would be traveling with around $7,000 in cash.

Our hope was that we would find Anna in Kyiv, because that would create the quickest adoption situation. However, in truth, she could be in any one of the 25 *oblasts* in Ukraine. It was just as likely that we would be spending our time in a rural village that had no access to modern conveniences as it was that we would be in a major city. Being unsure of where we were going only added to the stress. We really had no address that we could leave behind for our family. We rented an international cell phone that guaranteed coverage all over Ukraine. Still, we were going to the other side of the world, and we certainly couldn't just come running home in the case of emergencies.

As the days became less gray and grew bluer, the boys began to play outside, and I used the time to continue to prepare for the trip. With the windows open, I could hear the boys exploring bird nests and insect homes in our backyard.

Pausing from my work, I watched them play. Caught between the heartache of leaving them and my desire to find Anna, I could easily envision a beautiful little girl running around with them. Not knowing what Anna looked like, I often pictured a little girl with dark curly hair and big brown eyes. Sometimes, though, at times like that day, I pictured blonde hair that could catch the shine of the bright sun.

I tried to imagine what it would be like to finally meet her. We had been warned that she would probably be scared of us. She might not even want to leave the orphanage. Certainly, she would have no real idea of what was happening to her when she did meet us. I daydreamed, though, about a wonderful meeting of hearts.

My excitement was growing and, that day especially, I was full of hope. I had been given the name and phone number of a man who had, over ten years earlier, immigrated to the United States from Ukraine. At the time, Ukraine was still a part of the Soviet Union, and he and his family had left all that they knew to live here. They had traveled much the same road that was ahead of Anna, and I was grateful to have the chance to learn from him.

I finished my work and left the boys with Rob. I drove to the meeting place with the windows down on the car. The warm breeze felt good, and I had a tremendous peace about everything. We had seen God provide for us so generously, and I was certain that this man was another piece of encouragement.

We were set to leave in three days, and this meeting filled the need we had for some simple translations of captions for a photo album that we were taking with us. We wanted Anna's caregivers to be able to read to her the names of people and places in the pictures. As I approached the meeting place, I marveled at how prepared I actually felt.

When I did find the man, I am certain that I was glowing with excitement. As he worked on my album, he looked at me and smiled.

"You know," he said, "Ukrainians are atheists. We are all atheists by nature."

Offended, I merely smiled. He continued in his speech.

"You have no idea what you will find there. My son came to America with me when he was two. The change in culture traumatized him for months — and that was with parents who spoke his language. This child will not know what hit her. She will be nothing but confused...."

"Yes," I said, "but she will have a family."

"A family will not matter to her. She has never had a family and will not know what she is missing. You will be taking her from what she has always known and putting her someplace that she will never belong. You may mean well, but she will only know confusion."

He finished the translations, and, ironically, wished me luck on my endeavor. It was my first experience with what I have since heard referred to as that "melancholy Slavic spirit." It totally derailed my thinking.

Surely, she wants a family ... surely this is what is best for her!
I had never stopped to consider that maybe an adoption wouldn't

be in this child's best interest. *How could she not be better off with a family than in an orphanage?*

My mind was racing as I drove home. This entire adoption had been so difficult, and this bit of discouragement came when I least expected it. However, turning back was not an option at that point. Right or wrong, we were headed to Ukraine. But, as we made our final preparations to go, this final punch by the enemy deeply hurt.

Mother's Day 2002 was one of the most emotional Mother's Days I have ever had. Having hardly slept the night before, I was awake long before the sun rose. I quietly slipped out of bed and went out to sit on our deck.

As I watched the sunrise over the woods, I prayed.

I can't do it God. I can't get on an airplane and fly to the other side of the ocean with my boys back here — not knowing when I'll be coming back.

I sat and thought about the situation, and it all sank in. God was calling me to leave my boys for a time. He gave up his Son for 33 years. His Son was beaten, tortured, and crucified by the very people he came to rescue. I was leaving my sons for a matter of weeks in the loving care of their grandparents. The sacrifice that he was calling me to was one much smaller than the one that he himself made.

He understood the pain of what I was doing and the depth to which this sacrifice hurt. I knew, then, that he would care for Ben and Justin and that they would be ready for us to leave. With a prayer for strength and courage, tears in my eyes, and a hole in my heart, knowing it would be the last time I would do this for some time, I walked inside and woke the boys. It was time to get ready to go to the airport.

The contrast between the boys and me was almost comical. For every bit of pain I felt, they felt twice that much excitement. Too young to understand the concept of time, they were not concerned about how long we would be gone. They were only thinking about two things: lots of time with Grandma and Grandpa (which meant lots of candy) and their new baby sister.

My parents drove us to the airport. Once we pulled up to the curb, it was time to leave.

"Please take good care of them," I told my mom.

"You forget," she replied, "they are my babies, too."

I didn't want them to see me crying because they still did not understand that there was anything to be sad about. They knew that we were leaving, would be gone a while, and then would come back with their baby sister. They could see no reason for tears, and I did not want to give them one.

I hugged each one and told them I loved them. Then, as quickly as I could, I walked away. As soon as I was out of their line of vision, I dropped my baggage and sobbed, feeling as though a part of my heart had just been ripped from me. There were many difficult things I have been called to do, but, by far, leaving my boys was the most difficult thing I have ever done. Rob stood with me until I had finished crying. Then we picked up our bags and got in line to begin the process of flying to Ukraine.

The travel time to Ukraine was about sixteen hours, with a five-hour layover in Amsterdam. Our plane landed there at 6 a.m., so nothing, not even our wing of the airport, was open. We walked around the airport a bit, got some breakfast, and then went to camp out near our gate. Soon, a group of Americans came over and sat next to us.

"Are you headed to Ukraine, too?" one asked us.

"Yes," I replied. "We are going there to adopt. Have you been there before?"

"So many times," answered the lady. "We've gone on mission trips to the same area every spring for the past seven years ... I guess this is your first time, then?"

"Yes — and we really aren't sure what to expect."

"Well, I can tell you one thing — expect to wait for several hours at customs! As soon as you get off the plane, you'll follow a stairwell down to the basement. It'll fill up, almost immediately, with people wanting to get through customs. The line forms quickly and it takes at least a couple of hours to get through."

This was new information. I had emailed our contact the flight number and arrival time. However, I had not factored in two hours in customs. Did he know that it took that long?

Although I had checked into Calvary Chapel, there was only so much I knew about them. Ira, who was Ukrainian, was to be our translator and had been occasionally emailing with me to help me prepare documents and such. However, Jed, an American missionary serving Calvary Chapel Kyiv, was our main contact. All communication had been via email, and it had been somewhat sporadic right before we began to travel.

The more I thought about it, the more I couldn't shake the feeling that their facilitation program seemed too good to be true. It was so perfectly what we had been looking for, and it was so much cheaper than anything else we had found. Sure, there was a reason that it was so inexpensive (it was a ministry of the church), but still.... Although I was 99.9% certain that their program was all it purported to be, I could not be 100% certain until I met Jed and Ira.

Those thoughts consumed my mind as we waited for our plane. Not long before we left, Transparency International, a non-governmental agency devoted to combating corruption, released a study that showed poor results for Ukraine, ranking the country as one of the most corrupt countries in the world. This study had been showing up in almost every newspaper and news magazine that I (or, as it seemed, my father) picked up. We were willingly walking into a den of foxes, and we were walking there with thousands of dollars in cash.

As I sat there in the Amsterdam airport, far past the point of no return, I began to really worry. The Americans we had met were happily munching away on candy and chatting about the recent novels they had read. I, however, was sitting there worrying about what the future held for us.

A couple of hours later, we turned in our tickets for the flight and were herded with the rest of the passengers into a small waiting room. We waited in the cramped room for about fifteen minutes, although it was so hot, sweaty, and odorous that it felt like we were there for an hour. I was well aware that despite having traveled internationally before, I was headed into a country totally different than anything I had ever experienced.

Already exhausted, and simply too tired to fight my natural tendency in that direction, my mind completely succumbed to worry for the last leg of the trip. I didn't even talk to Rob, whose tendency to focus on what could go wrong was not only stronger than mine, but much more creative as well. For over an hour and half, I worried about who we were working with, where our home would be, how safe our boys were, and if they missed us yet. And, I worried about how we would get through customs.

"You must fill out this form," the stewardess handed a small slip of paper to me as her heavily accented voice interrupted my thoughts, "You will need it to get through customs — both into and out of the country. It is very important. Do not lose it."

The paper was short, but hardly simple. There were words in English, Russian, Ukrainian, and several other languages. I wrote my name on the first blank, and then realized that I was supposed to write my last name first. I scribbled it out and rearranged the order.

No, no, I thought, *I had it right the first time.*

I scratched it out again, and rewrote it.

No, that will never work, now it looks like I am trying to hide something since I keep changing my name...

The stewardess gave me another form, and I started again. When the next attempt went just as badly, I called the stewardess again. She nicely gave me several forms — just in case.

I got down to the last question: "How much money do you carry on your person?"

"$3,500 US dollars," I wrote, already uneasy at having to admit what I was carrying. I gripped the customs form and my passport like an elderly woman would hold her purse while riding a city bus. In my mind, I was surrounded by possible thieves. They only *looked* like families, businessmen, humanitarian aid workers, and Ukrainian citizens headed home for a visit.

The plane began its descent, and I began to think entirely too much. My Russian language instruction consisted of a half-finished course of "Russian in 10 Minutes a Day." Rob had an entire semester of college Russian under his belt. How in the world were we going to navigate customs and passport control in Ukraine?

I am really trusting in your goodness and mercy on this one, God. I prayed.

The plane landed and slowly came to a stop. I looked at Rob.

"Are you ready?" I asked, knowing that whatever lay outside the plane was vastly different than anything we had ever done together. I was also well aware of the fact that, no matter how things worked out while we were here, our lives were about to drastically change.

"As ready as I'm ever going to be," he replied.

We exited the plane and walked off the ramp and into a cinderblock hallway that led to a stairwell. We followed the stairwell down further and further into the dark. I began to wonder if we were lost. We were among the first people to leave the plane and we were not positive we were even headed in the right direction. It certainly didn't seem like a customs or passport control office. The stairwell led to a cinderblock basement.

The hallway opened up into a large room, with scanty light, no windows, several x-ray machines, and a conveyor belt for luggage. We had arrived at customs.

Standing directly inside the doorway was a tall man dressed in some type of airline uniform (dark pants, white dress shirt, and a name tag). His dark hair was slicked off his forehead, almost in the manner of an Elvis impersonator. He had a foreboding scowl on his face and a cigarette hanging out of his mouth. As he glared at the people headed toward the room, he was holding something — a sign.

Great, I thought, *the first thing we encounter is a large, burly man holding a sign we can't read! It could say "Do not enter!" or "No Americans allowed!" for all I know. I really should have finished that Russian in 10 Minutes a Day course!*

As we approached the doorway, the sign became clearer. It said one word and one word only: AMEND.

I was so confused. I stopped and stared at the man. Was this ... *Jed*? I had seen a picture of him on Calvary Chapel Kyiv's website, but I couldn't really recall what he looked like. This was not what I had pictured. And I never would have guessed him to be a smoker!

"Jed" threw down his cigarette and yelled over to us.

"You ... Amend?"

"Yes ..." we cautiously answered. Who was this man?

"Jed. Jed sent me." His accent was heavy.

We nodded in understanding, even though we were truly clueless.

"Take pencil and fill out paper as I say." He handed us pencils.

"Okay. Go ... Name, USA ... no ... no ... no ... no ... yes." He was rapidly pointing at various spots on the paper. He was instructing us so quickly we could not even read what the questions on the form were. I was so confused, should I answer "No" or "Nyet"? "Yes" or "Da"? And, still, who was this man anyway?

No time for contemplation, though, as "Jed" interrupted my thoughts.

"Quickly! Quickly! Fill in as I tell you and you will beat the line!"

Then we got it. We did what he said, and he raced us over to the luggage conveyor belt.

"You stay here and get suitcase. I get you spot in line for passport officer."

He ran off to save us a spot in the passport control line, and we obeyed him and waited for our luggage. I was relieved when the luggage was returned intact. We lugged it off the conveyor belt and dragged it all over to passport control.

There were two passport agents, and each worked at his own kiosk. Although the number of people going through customs was growing exponentially, the passport agents were not in any hurry. Their conversation bounced back and forth, with hands waving, faces smiling, and loud laughter. We waited patiently, as they slowly checked the passports of the handful of people in front of us.

Unable to go through together, Rob let me go first (which I am sure he did in order to be a gentleman, not to have me be the test run for the interviews). In the end, though, he went to the other agent at the same time I was interviewed.

"Why are you here?" the agent asked.

"To adopt," I said, the $3,500 split between two money belts was burning holes in my chest and side.

He looked at the information on my customs report. His eyes took on a certain mystical glow when he saw the amount of cash I was carrying.

"I will need to see your cash."

I had my suspicions. The last thing that I wanted to do was get out my money belts and show him my money. I looked him straight in the eye.

"The money is in my shirt. I don't think that would be appropriate."

There was a pregnant pause in the conversation. Then, he smiled at me.

"You are right," he said. And, with that, he stamped my passport.

Rob, however, was not faring so well. His agent looked over his customs form, and he, too, smiled.

"I would like to see your cash."

Unable to point out the impropriety of sticking his hand in his shirt and pulling out money, Rob complied. He took out the $3,500 and counted it for the man.

"I will need to look at it," he told Rob.

Now, it was obvious, from the start, that he did not need to look at it, but he certainly did love to hold it. He stood there, holding the $3,500 for about thirty seconds, fanning it, smelling it and, well, caressing it. Then he called my agent over, who proceeded to do the same. $3,500, well more than the average Ukrainian earns in an entire year, in small, unmarked bills certainly had an impact on these men.

"Looks good," he said, and he handed the money back to Rob.

It was almost like we had been privy to an intimate moment. He stamped Rob's passport and sent us along.

Meanwhile, our mystery man was calling to us again. There was a large set of frosted glass sliding doors at the front of the room. He was barreling, with my suitcase in tow, toward those doors. I followed him, calling out for Rob.

"Wait," Rob replied. "I have to put the cash back in the money belt ..." and with that the sliding glass doors opened to the main concourse of the airport where, literally, hundreds of Ukrainians were standing. They all seemed to be looking in one direction — at my husband — the man standing there waving $3,500 in cash.

And that is how we officially arrived in Ukraine.

Kyiv

Ukraine's glory hasn't perished, nor her freedom
Upon us, fellow compatriots, fate shall smile once more.
Our enemies will vanish, like dew in the morning sun,
And we too shall rule, brothers, in a free land of our
*   own.*

We'll lay down our souls and bodies to attain our
*   freedom,*
And we'll show that we, brothers, are of the Kozak
*   nation.*

— Ukrainian National Anthem

O afflicted city, lashed by storms and not comforted, I
will build you with stones of turquoise, your founda-
tions with sapphires. I will make your battlements of
rubies, your gates of sparkling jewels, and all your walls
of precious stones. All your sons will be taught by the
Lord, and great will be your children's peace.

— Isaiah 54:11-13 (NIV)

After entering the main concourse, we finally met the real Jed. I was very relieved to find that he was not anything like the man we met coming off the airplane. Jed had brought with him another member of the church, a young woman, tall, with blonde hair and blue eyes. She had a friendly smile, and we were immediately comfortable with her.

"I am Olya." Her accent made her voice beautiful. "I will be helping you with your adoption. Ira will do most of the work, but she was unable to meet you today."

Any fears I had about who was helping us completely diminished the moment we met Jed and Olya. We were welcomed so warmly and instantly felt like we had known Jed and Olya for years. It is amazing how the church is like that, family despite the fact that we had never physically met before that moment. To this day, people have asked me many questions about Calvary Chapel that I simply cannot answer.

- "Do they speak in tongues?"
- "Do they baptize children?"
- "What translation of the Bible do they use?"
- "Are they young earth creationists?"

None of the questions have answers because none of that really matters. When you work with Christians in the real world, you don't care so much about specific church doctrine. You are just people united by the need to continue following Christ.

We left the airport and stepped out into the warm Ukrainian sun. As we walked to Jed's van, I tried to take it all in. The parking lot was full of old, boxy European cars. So full, that the cars were triple parked everywhere. But the uniqueness and number of the cars paled in comparison to the driving.

Jed raced the church van down the street, and we, unsuccessfully, looked for seatbelts. A strong breeze cooled us off as we sped along, swaying at U-turns, changing lanes, and even changing direction mid-lane. I have been to Europe before, and I understand that Europeans drive differently than Americans. In fact, I have had the pleasure of riding in cars on three different continents, and

I can say with great certainty, *"No one in the world drives like Ukrainians."* The amount of time we had spent traveling by air was much greater than that 45-minute ride to our apartment. But I am uncertain which had the greater risk.

Our new home was located in a housing subdivision called Teremki. Nearly all of the housing in Kyiv is divided into subdivisions of apartment complexes. Teremki was a moderately large subdivision with approximately ten or so tall apartment buildings. They were built in groups of three or more, with playgrounds and grassy lawns woven together by sidewalks that connected them and the buildings. Although they appeared much older, the oldest buildings were built in the 1970s. We were told that ownership of individual apartments had been granted to Soviet citizens as rewards for years of service as workers, with some of the younger buildings having been constructed in the late 1980s in order to house displaced families from the Chernobyl disaster.

Our building, painted white, with cracks cutting through the façade in every direction, was about eighteen stories tall. Windows and balconies broke up the monotony of the building, while splashes of color from the clothes lines hanging in the balconies added life to what looked like a deserted place. A sidewalk, broken, cracked, and surrounded by knee-high grass, snaked away from the main entrance and led to both the parking lot and a small playground that I investigated as our luggage was being unloaded.

From a distance, it looked like any playground that I had ever taken the boys to: a slide, several swings, and a teeter-totter. Up close, though, I could see how much work it needed. The equipment was painted metal, although there appeared to be more rust than paint. There were jagged edges, pieces missing, and nails sticking out. At first, I was considering it as a place to play with Anna, however, once I looked at it, I winced at the thought of allowing my children to play on it.

My wince bothered me, though my reaction was almost involuntary as I compared this playground to the safety inspected playground that the children play on at home.

If it was *good enough for the children who lived there, certainly it* was *good enough for my children*, I thought as the guilt of my own personal affluence contrasted with a society full of poverty shadowed my mood.

Concrete steps paved the way to the main entrance, which was marked by heavy metal doors, painted a dark orange to match the design of the building. An elderly matron (a throw over from Soviet days when each apartment building had an employee keep tabs on the comings and goings of the residents) greeted us when we entered.

The lobby was entirely cinderblock. The floor was uneven, and each doorway was covered by a thin metal door spotted with rust. There was little light, most of it coming from the door leading to the outside. The matron sat in a chair in a small windowed office, peeking out over the top of a dutch door.

Jed suggested that we use the elevator since we had our luggage with us. I was not too sure. What I had seen of the building so far certainly did not indicate structural soundness. The four of us (and all of our luggage) entered the elevator. The door slowly closed, and, just when I thought that it couldn't get any darker ... it did. The faint light in the elevator barely illuminated the buttons, which did not matter much since all the numbers had been worn off them. Our apartment, though, was on the second floor, an easy guess. Even in the dark.

The elevator painfully inched its way up one floor, sighing and creaking all the way, and opened to reveal yet another cinderblock hallway with concrete floors and very little light. To me, the inside of this Soviet-designed building felt like catacombs, leading to three doors, each one positioned to take us in a completely different direction. The only light in the hallway came from an open balcony that was situated outside one of the doors.

The door directly in front of us led to our hallway and clanked behind us as we slowly made our way toward our new home. This hallway, illuminated by one light hanging down from a wire in the ceiling, was the darkest yet. There were three doors in the hall, and ours was on the side that faced the front of the building. Olya unlocked two locks on the door and opened it to reveal a second door. She undid another lock, that door swung open, and we were in our home.

70

"Please always keep the doors locked, even when you are here," Olya said quietly as she stepped out of her shoes and shut the door behind her.

The doorway entered into a spacious foyer. The foyer led to three rooms, all of which faced the front of the building. To the right were two closed doors that led to the bathrooms. Soviet bathrooms were designed with function in mind. One bathroom housed the bathtub and sink, and the other housed the toilet. I quickly found out that the rumors I had heard about the quality of Ukrainian toilet paper were all true. It was function, not comfort, that dictated the use of their bathrooms.

The kitchen was small. Placed next to the balcony window was a table just big enough for Rob and me to sit. Squeezed next to one side was a small, old stove next to about a foot of counter space. There were cabinets with dishes and a small sink, too. The refrigerator, located on the opposite side of the table, was as tall as my shoulders. The kitchen was stocked with some food and water for us; another symbol of the care they took in welcoming us.

Starting the second night the kitchen faucet began to drip. By the third night the dripping became loud enough that we thought one of us must not have turned it off correctly. I went in to the kitchen and turned the knob. Sure enough, it stopped. I turned around and started to leave the kitchen, but before I could leave, I heard the dripping again. I slowly turned around and looked at the sink.

Drip ...... drip ….. drip …. drip ... drip ... drip .. drip .. drip ..

I walked back over and turned it off. The scene then repeated itself several more times. Finally, determined to win this little battle, I got out our role of duct tape. I walked back into the kitchen, turned the sink off and duct taped the handle in that position by duct taping around it and then to the wall — a very handy fix.

Thinking I had won, I decided to go to bed. The moment my head hit the pillow though, I knew that my sleep would be disturbed. There was one little sound.

Drip.

Several minutes later I heard it again.

Drip.

Each minute it grew with intensity and frequency. Then, we both shot out of bed, when we heard an amazing sound. The faucet was running! We ran into the kitchen to see what happened. The sink was running just as though someone had turned it on. Within minutes we had an explanation: The inside of the cold water handle was stripped, and whenever anything rattled the plumbing lines (including our neighbors flushing the toilet), it simply slipped on.

I duct taped it again and went to bed. Within minutes, the faucet was running again. The faucet ran, without stopping, the entire time we were in Ukraine. Despite the fact that we kept mentioning to people that it needed fixed, it is probably still running to this day. I quickly learned that, in Ukraine, one severely leaky faucet was not on the top of any fix-it man's list.

The other two rooms were combination living room/bedrooms. The beds were covered with heavy woolen blankets and rugs. Rugs hung on the walls and covered the hardwood floors. The only windows faced the front of the building with balconies outside each of the main rooms.

It was clean, dry, and warm, and it was, at least temporarily, home.

I never understood jet lag until our first night in Ukraine. We had spent the evening dining out with Jed, his family, and some other members of the church. After arriving home, Rob was exhausted and had no problem falling asleep. For me, however, sleep was evasive. I lay in bed, exhausted, but unable to even keep my eyes closed.

I wonder what the boys are doing right now, I thought. I envisioned our second story deck dramatically falling off the house while Justin and Ben innocently played on it. *Did I remember to tell my mom not give Justin hard candy? What if they are riding their bikes into the street? What about stray dogs? What about car seats, seat belts, and kidnappers?* I tossed, turned, and worried about the boys. Then, I moved onto the next problem: us.

What was that noise? Is someone trying to get into our apartment? We are so vulnerable here by ourselves! The truth of the matter was that we had phone numbers for several different families that we could call in case of an emergency, including a family that lived in the same building as us. But my mind continued racing as I lay there trying to fall asleep. The bed was completely different than what I was used to: a thin mattress covered with itchy wool blankets that felt like rugs. They were covered in sheets, but sometimes the sheet would pull away and the heavy wool would scratch my skin. The bed even smelled different, and, because of that it felt unclean to me. Finally, I decided that it was a battle I was not going to win. I quietly slipped out of the room, grabbed a book, and read until 3:30 in the morning.

I slept lightly and awoke early in the morning with Rob next to me, sleeping like a log. It was completely beyond me how he could still be sleeping. Some people's internal clocks just don't get turned around.

Even though the night's sleep was terrible, I was rested enough to start my day. I was finally in Ukraine, and I was ready to fill my eyes with as many sights as I could. It was so exciting to me. Years ago, I had studied a collection of piano music by Modest Mussorgsky called *Pictures at An Exhibition*. The ending piece of the collection is called "The Great Gate of Kyiv," and ever since I'd studied it I wanted to see the city. I was ready to go, but unfortunately it was hours until Olya was to show up to take us sightseeing. And, by the looks of things, it would be hours until I would even be able to enjoy the company of my husband. So, I decided to take a look around.

The apartment was full of what my children would call treasures, things not worth much for their monetary value, but valuable because of their uniqueness. The cabinets had the usual dried beans, pasta, and cooking mixes. I studied each package, deciphering the Cyrillic enough to figure out where it had been made (Germany, Turkey, Israel ...). Then I moved on to the dishes. Most looked like dishes we would use at home, but I continued to look for something unusual, and, I finally found it: A cup. In fact, I was even tempted to pocket it.

It was a small teacup with a delicate handle and a small chip in the side of it. On the front was the familiar hammer and sickle symbol of the Soviet Union. I deciphered the Cyrillic enough to figure out that the cup was designed to celebrate the fiftieth anniversary of the Soviet Union. It was an odd feeling to study an object that celebrated a regime now known to be so evil and to realize that a few decades earlier where I stood would've have been considered enemy territory in the cold war.

I stared out the window taking in the Cyrillic writing on buildings and signs and looking at the landscapes. We were surrounded by buildings that looked almost exactly like ours, tall grass surrounding each one and juxtaposed to the construction of a half-completed building across the street. As I took it all in, I had to confess to myself that it reminded me of the housing projects from home, yet, in some instances, in even less repair. As the sun rose, though, the place became alive with people, and it was in the people that I saw the difference. The people leaving the buildings and going to work (difference number one!) were dressed in professional clothing. Many of these people were college educated professionals, people who, if they lived in America, would be living in nice homes in the suburbs.

I watched as the people streamed out of our building and off to work, often dropping a bag of trash into the dumpster in our parking lot. After a time, the flow of people slowed, and before long, a little babushka hobbled into the lot. Walking with a limp, she used a cane to steady her gate. Her gray coat was buttoned up to her throat and a colorful scarf covered her head. She carried a plastic grocery bag with her. I watched as she slowly made her way across the parking lot and to the dumpster. Then, after struggling to open the lid, she began to dig through, picking out leftover food and placing it in her bag. After searching through the morning trash for several minutes, she closed the lid and slowly hobbled down the street. I watched as she walked away and pondered the life of a person who was forced to pick through trash to find food. She returned each morning at the same time, every day that we were in Kyiv, a somber reminder of how difficult life there was.

74

The Dnieper River snakes through the middle of Kyiv continuing north and south, dividing not only the city, but the entire country into an east and west, until it reaches the Black Sea. It seemed as though no matter where we went in the city, be it the World War II Museum, the Afghanistan War Memorial, or the beautiful orthodox Pechersk Lavra, the placid river provided a beautiful background to the view.

"There was a large war in Europe, back in the 1940s," Olya began to tell us as we entered the World War II Museum. "There were some very evil men from Germany...."

We smiled as we explained to her that we knew all about the war in America, too, and pointed out that the USA had actually joined in as the war neared its end. But as we walked past the first exhibit, a sculpture of a Nazi Eagle with the wings snapped off lying on either side of the bird's body, and into a gallery filled with photos of the Nazi Regime, I began to realize the depth to which Ukraine had been hurt by not only WWII, but the Soviet Regime as well. "The Allies won the war," noted American Journalist Edgar Snow after viewing the destruction done by the Nazi occupation, "but Ukraine paid the bill" — a fact long-hidden from the world as it was in the Soviet Union's best interest to celebrate "Russia's sacrifice" rather than revealing which Soviet state gave the most. Long before Hitler ever marched his troops onto Ukrainian soil and slaughtered millions, Stalin's torturous reign had already starved over eight million Ukrainians to death, as he exported to Moscow the wealth of what was referred to as the USSR's breadbasket.

In exchange for the years of servitude Ukraine was given the famous Motherland Statue that overlooks the Dnieper River, near the World War II Museum. Before traveling, we had read that controversy surrounded the statue as to whether it was a benevolent gift given to celebrate the birthplace of the Kyivien-Rus culture, or a nice reminder of the Russian Motherland watching over the city of Kyiv.

It was hard for me to even begin to form an opinion of the statue's meaning when everything looked so extreme. Outside the WWII Museum was the monument to the Afghanistan War, and as I viewed it, the intensity of the faces of the soldiers in the monument (in combination with the dark and passionate music that played in the background) contrasted in my mind the great war monuments at home — ones that seemed to have much more light about them. The Russian soldiers did not even seem to belong to the same league as "our boys" back home! I began to realize how my own biases shaped how I was viewing my future daughter's homeland, and I prayed that God would open my mind to the beauty of Ukrainian culture.

We spent the remainder of our day indulging in the bounty of Ukrainian cuisine, sipping warm cokes, trying *borsch*, *blini*, dumplings, cabbage soup, and mushroom sauce.

We experienced the sincerity the Ukrainian orthodoxy when we visited Pechersk Lavra and watched as many families reverently placed flowers on the tombs of the preserved bodies of saints from long ago. We also enjoyed bartering with local peddlers as we attempted to buy souvenirs.

At the end of the day, we returned home exhausted. We had seen the beauty of Kyiv, the spirit of a people not defeated by a history of human rights violations and dictators, a land that still created a beautiful landscape, and a culture opening itself up to the materialism of the west. It had been a day of contrasts: lasting beauty and a history of destruction, wonderful exotic food at restaurants and people begging for bread in the streets, bartering with street vendors and seeing advertisements for McDonald's, committed orthodox believers and atheistic Soviet propaganda.

I was overwhelmed by the complexity of where I was and ready to move on to the next step leading home.

The National Adoption Center

Every child is precious, every child is a gift from God.

Saying there are too many children is like saying there are too many flowers.

— Mother Teresa of Calcutta

One day, children were brought to Jesus in the hope that he would lay hands on them and pray over them. The disciples shooed them off. But Jesus intervened: "Let the children alone, don't prevent them from coming to me. God's kingdom is made up of people like these." — Matthew 19:13-14 (The Message)

Once again regretting the lack of seatbelts in the car, I looked at Ira, our translator, as our driver weaved in and out of traffic. She had absolutely no reaction. Not even as he crossed over into the lane with oncoming traffic, in order to pass a slow-moving bus. Another reminder that we weren't in the US anymore!

It was early Wednesday morning, our third day away from home, and we were headed for the first official step in our adoption, a visit to the National Adoption Center (NAC), the federal government's adoption hub. Ukraine is divided into 25 *oblasts* (regions). When a child enters an orphanage in Ukraine, a file of paperwork for them is established. The orphanage compiles documents relating to the birth family, abandonment, birth certificates, medical records, and such. They then send paperwork on to their oblast's government. The paperwork will stay with the oblast government for a period of time, and if no member of the birth family has expressed any interest, the paperwork is sent to the NAC. In all, the child has to be available for adoption by Ukrainian families for about one year before being made available for international adoption.

The exceptions to the wait are children with serious special needs. These children, historically more difficult to place, are available for international adoption from the day they are placed in the orphanage. Though they my be legally available from the start, no one may know about them for years — until their paperwork makes its way through the bureaucratic maze all the way to Kyiv.

For months, I had been biting my nails about our first trip to the NAC. Communication with other families that had been through the process had enlightened us to the process we were facing and the two people that we had to meet with there. The first person was the director, infamous because we had heard horror stories about her. According to the members of the adoption email groups we had joined, there was no way to predict how she would react to you.

And, since we had obviously never met her, we had no idea what to expect. In light of the struggle we had already had, we expected the worst.

The infertility rate in Ukraine is relatively high. As that rate has increased, there has actually been a decline in the population, and that decline has led more and more Ukrainians to adopt babies. The result is that fewer babies are available for adoption by foreigners. While it was certainly an answer to the prayers of many people, it has caused a shift in the adoption situation. Ukraine, once a popular place to adopt healthy infants, is no longer a country in need of that. When we arrived, the children available for adoption were either older children or children with serious special needs.

The problem was that agencies in the United States were not communicating this to their prospective families. They were still sending families hoping to find a healthy baby in Ukraine. I believed that the director was at her wit's end dealing with these shocked families. That was my theory. It was a theory I liked because it gave me reason to believe we would not endure any of the wrath that other families had. I later learned that this director was arrested on charges of selling babies to American couples, so perhaps my naïveté was greater than I realized.

We arrived at the National Adoption Center at about 8:30 a.m. I was surprised by the building, which was little more than a small four- or five-story brownstone. The concrete steps were worn unevenly and the stairwell was dark. We walked up several flights of steps, and I noted that the air was stagnant. There was no air conditioning in the building, which at that early hour, was already uncomfortable. We got to the top of the stairs, turned down the hallway, and were stopped by a line of about fifty people. It was my first experience with a Ukrainian line. The office had just opened and the line went all the way down the hallway. There were three or four different doors, so it was difficult for us to see which people were in line for which door.

"The director's office is at the end of the hall," Ira told us.

"We are in for a long wait," I noted.

"No ... not too bad," she smiled.

We waited. And waited and waited until noon. Ira inched her way up the hall to find out why the line was not moving. Rob and I stood there waiting. The hallway was filled well beyond any safe capacity, and I was surprised by not only the amount of people, but the variety.

There was a family from Germany with a little boy, dressed in lederhosen, and a white shirt, his head capped by a green hat with a feather. Playing with his dad, I could occasionally hear him giggle and say, *"Ich liebe mein Papa!"* There was an Italian couple holding an elaborate bouquet of flowers and bottles of wine. My eavesdropping brought us the knowledge that those items were for the director — we, of course, were empty-handed. Ira had assured us we should bring the gifts after the adoption was completed. That way they were gifts, not bribes. However, I was annoyed that we were obviously not playing on an even playing field.

Most of the families, however, were American. Some were in line for their interview. Nervous and tired from travel, they, like us, were excited about what lay ahead. It was the other families that worried me. The ones who were there for the third or fourth time in the past week. These families had picked children to meet, traveled to meet them, and had found them unacceptable to adopt. When that is the case, the family is sent back to the NAC to choose another child to visit. The tears were flowing, and these were not happy people. Due to the recent changes in children available, there were a lot of them, and I couldn't help but wonder if that was where Rob and I would find ourselves in the next week or so.

As I pondered these things, Ira returned to us full of information. There was a news crew interviewing Mrs. Kunko and doing a news story on the NAC. Apparently someone important, an ambassador or public figure of some sort, was beginning the process to adopt. The news crew was just finishing up and would be leaving shortly. The line would then begin to move.

At 11:59 we were standing outside the office door with one family ahead of us. The director stuck her head out the door. She saw Ira, and they talked for a few moments. Then she yelled down the hall. I looked at the faces of all the translators, and guessed, from the fallen expressions, what she said.

Ira, however, looked pretty happy.

"She's going to lunch," Ira smiled, "but not until after she interviews you. We are the last interview she will conduct today. All those behind us were just told to come back tomorrow!"

Relaxed, but nervous, we waited those last few minutes. Finally, it was time for our interview. Shaking from nerves, we entered the room.

She looked at us, and indicated for us to sit.

"Your names are Robert and Deborah Amend?" Ira translated.

"Yes."

"You wish to adopt from Ukraine?"

"Yes."

"You are US citizens?"

"Yes."

"All your paperwork has been properly submitted?"

"Yes."

"Come back tomorrow to start reviewing files of children. Good-bye."

That was it. Months of worry and agony over the "interview" and it was a perfunctory fifteen-second quiz. We were so relieved. We went out to lunch to celebrate that first tiny accomplishment and then headed back to our apartment to rest and prepare for the next step. In the meantime, Ira went about getting all the appropriate stamps and letters that we needed to move down the hallway to the next room. There, we would meet with a state psychologist and begin the process of selecting a child.

Day four saw us back at the NAC at 8:30 a.m. again. And, once again, there was a long queue filling the now very familiar hallway. There was a real sense of apprehension about us, though, as this was the day that we would pick a child to meet. All around us were unhappy couples who, unable to find an "appropriate child" to adopt, were back to pick their third or fourth child to meet. It seemed that everywhere I looked people were crying and arguing. I was so worried that we would not find a child, especially since young girls were not as numerous as boys. We knew that the real battle was just beginning, and we were uncertain as to what would happen next.

We stood waiting in the hallway until it was our turn. We walked in and sat down at the desk of one of the psychologists. She began talking and Ira began translating.

"We have many children available for adoption. Especially older children. We have so many boys age five and over and so many girls age seven and up that do not have families. So before we start, promise me that when you go home, you will tell your friends, your church, and your family about all the beautiful children in Ukraine that need to be adopted."

We promised.

Then she asked us, "What are you looking for?"

We answered, "A girl, age three or under, and we are very open to special needs."

"How about this little girl?" She thrust a picture and medical page at us.

I looked at the picture and could not believe what I saw. There was a little girl looking straight at me, smiling. I heard Rob gasp.

"She looks like my dad," he said.

Ira translated the medical information for us. She was just over three years old, and in generally good health. They said she was exceptionally bright and her only special need was that her right hand was fused to her leg.

"Well," Rob noted, "It would make for interesting diaper changes."

The psychologist handed us some other pictures and files. We felt obligated to look. The children drew so much compassion and pity from us. We looked first in Kyiv, as that would mean the quickest adoption since there would be no extra travel. Rob flipped open the binder. The first picture was a beautiful seven-year-old girl. She had long curly blonde hair and big blue eyes. Her beauty was overwhelming, and we couldn't contain our shock over the fact that she was available for adoption. However, she was too old for us to consider, as we did not feel called to disrupt the birth order of our family. Then followed child after child from Kyiv: Down's syndrome, hydrocephaly, cancer, blindness, and hepatitis. Though they were so compelling, none seemed to be the right fit for our family.

"Well," said Ira, "if we are going to travel, where would you like to go?"

"The Black Sea — Odessa," I replied. If I was going to be stuck some place for a while, I figured that I would like to be stuck at a beach.

"We can try that, but it is a seaport so it presents a problem of its own."

I opened the binder, and, from the first page I could guess what the problem was. Each page, page after page, had pictures of beautiful little children, and, almost every page had three big letters written boldly at the top: HIV. My heart was broken, I couldn't look at anymore. I closed the binder, completely aware that there were still over twenty more binders full of children.

Rob and I both looked at the original child we were given. I asked the psychologist, "Where is she?"

"Vinnitsa ... I can phone the orphanage and make sure she is still there and everything is in line with the information that we have here, if you would like."

We waited while she phoned. A wall map of Ukraine hung near the psychologist's desk. Ira showed us where Vinnitsa was. Located only about 300 kilometers southwest of Kyiv, I decided that traveling there would not add too much time onto our stay in Ukraine. I truly was hopelessly naive.

The director finished her conversation with the orphanage and then explained it all to Ira. She translated for us.

"She is still there, and her hand has already been surgically detached from her leg. It is slightly smaller than her left hand and does not work well. Other than that they said she is just wonderful. They all love her, and she is very smart."

That was enough for us. We decided to go visit this little girl whose name was Halyna. I, of course, still naive in my understanding of Ukraine, was ready to walk out the door, hire a driver, and go meet her. But, this was Ukraine, and we still had to get all the right documents to show we had permission to meet her. While we were busy packing our suitcases, Ira spent the rest of the day getting the remaining stamps necessary for us to go to Vinnitsa.

Anna Halyna

What are little girls made of?
Sugar and spice
And everything nice.
That's what little girls are made of.
                    — Traditional nursery rhyme

Grace was in all her steps. Heaven in her eye. In every
gesture, dignity and love.
                    — John Milton, *Paradise Lost*

I prayed for this child, and the Lord has granted me
what I asked of him.   — 1 Samuel 1:27 (NIV)

The bus was very, very old. The sun glistened on its brown and
tan sides. I doubted that there was air conditioning and noted that
none of the windows were opened.

"Our luggage goes back here," Ira said, as she walked to the
back of the bus. We slid our bags on and watched as a box of chicks
was placed next to a cat carrier. I paused with wonder at what the

ride would be like. However, 300 kilometers should only take a few hours, and that would be easy to endure.

The seats of the bus were a faded red and brown, possibly at one time velour. The windows had dainty beige curtains to shade us from the sun. It was incredibly hot, though it was still early in the morning. We found some seats and settled in. Ira opened our window and hers. As soon as she sat down, a little babushka in the seat in front of us popped up, leaned back over her seat, and closed our window with great ferocity. Like many eastern Europeans, she did not trust the effect that wind could have on a person. Ira noticed the window was again closed, so, before sitting down, she opened it once more. With unexpected lightning speed, the babushka jumped up and slammed it shut. I knew that I was certainly not going to have a showdown with her no matter how hot I got. So the window stayed shut.

As the bus filled, I turned around and asked Ira when we would arrive in Vinnitsa.

"Sometime after lunch, perhaps between 1:00 and 2:00."

The bus was pulling out as I calculated the time. It was exactly 7 a.m., so that would mean ... six to seven hours on this bus! How could it take six to seven hours to drive about 150 miles?

I settled in, adjusted to the long ride, and decided to enjoy the sights. I knew that I only had this one chance to memorize my child's birth country. Looking out the window as we drove through Kyiv, and then out into the countryside and through villages, I began to grasp bits and pieces of what life was like in this country.

In the city, small kiosks were everywhere. People sold things not to build up IRAs or pay for second cars, but in order to buy food. A college professor might teach and research throughout the week and then sell his woodwork on the downtown square on the weekends. People sold kittens, puppies, flowers, clothes, umbrellas, food, baby items, and anything else they thought might have a buyer. Once, when riding the metro, I watched as a man dressed in a suit stepped on, set his things down as the door closed, and grabbed a handful of ink pens out of a brown paper bag.

"I've got some pens here, if you are in need!" he yelled. "Good price, high quality. Will not leak on your shirt." He said as he clicked the pen in and out over and over again. His sales pitch continued for his entire ride, then he dropped the pens back into the brown paper bag, grabbed his belongings, and left. He had not sold a single pen, but my guess is that he would try again the next time he rode the subway.

The kiosks were lined up near the street, unless there was grass there. Wherever there was grass, there was a small vegetable garden. This was so within the city limits, and as we drove to the outskirts, it became even more common. Soon, when we were out in the country, the kiosks were rare, but the gardens plentiful and it was not long before we saw our first full-fledged farm.

Almost lost in the middle of a huge field was a little old lady, her gray hair pulled back with a scarf and her skirt swaying in the wind, working the soil with one hoe. I watched as she meticulously turned the soil, her back hunched over the hoe, inching her way across the field. The soil looked so fresh and rich, like the soil at home looked when I had worked with it, watering it, adding fertilizer to it, and turning it. However, at home, the soil would soon turn brown and hard, but this soil was always this black and lush. The famous breadbasket of the Soviet Union, Ukraine's soil is capable of producing some of the most delicious produce in the world.

Between the field and the highway, the farmer had staked his two cows and a couple of goats. A precious commodity to him, the animals were kept near his home. The home itself appeared abandoned. There was no glass in the windows and no wiring into the house. However, the animals, clothing hung out to dry, and farm tools lying about showed that this house was, indeed, inhabited.

I had time to study all this, because, our bus driver had stopped the bus at a small kiosk near the farm. While the kiosks in the city sold food, clothes, and other necessities, an enterprising young man had opened up one on this highway that sold something uniquely necessary for this leg of the trip: air freshener. We were several hours into the trip, and the bus, with very few open windows, a full capacity of people and animals, was filled with unusual odors. Tired, nervous, and feeling sick from all the odors, I was drifting in and out of sleep.

That was when the bus slowed to a stop and the bus driver stepped out. He walked up to the kiosk and settled in for a full sales pitch. The salesman held up the first option, an aerosol freshener. He sprayed a pinch. The bus driver sniffed and shook his head. So, the salesman showed him the next, with a delicate spray. The driver shook his head no. He tried a third; still no.

Then the driver picked up a Christmas-tree-shaped hanging air freshener. Some bickering occurred, and then money changed hands. The driver returned, quite pleased with his purchase, hung the refreshing tree on his review mirror, and we continued on our way.

I was beginning to understand how a 300-kilometer trip could take seven hours.

Finally, we arrived in Vinnitsa. The bus station was located on the same side of town as the orphanage, and we were able to quickly find a cab to drive us there. Ira explained to us our current situation. It was Friday, and the orphanage director would be leaving for the weekend within the next couple of hours. Time was of the essence, because if we missed the director, then we could not get her permission to meet the girl. If that happened, then we would have to wait until Monday to meet her. If we met her that afternoon and decided we did not want to adopt her, then we could head back to Kyiv the next morning and be ready to pick a new child on Monday.

The cab turned onto a bumpy back road that ran along the backsides of eight to ten houses. We entered a gate that opened to the orphanage ground, and, for the first time, I saw the building that my daughter had called home.

White stone with some sky blue accent paint, the baby house looked very much like an institution. There was nothing that marked it as a place for children, except the old playground surrounded by knee-high grass. Three large dogs, with long black fur, were digging through the garbage that overflowed to cover the area around the cans. The building, surrounded by a cement path, had several doorways, each one accessed by uneven, chipped concrete steps. Voices of children drifted out of the building through windows that were missing glass.

We told our cabby to wait and then entered the orphanage. A peculiar odor wafted past us, and I later figured out that it was a combination of bleach from cleaning mixed with the smell of stewed cabbage. The hallway was long and lit by the sunlight coming through the windows. Twists and turns in the building disoriented me as we were led to the director's office. There, we waited for several minutes until she entered the room.

Nina Svetlanova was a tall, middle-aged woman with graying blonde hair and glasses. Large boned and loud voiced, her demeanor was foreboding. When she began her conversation with Ira, at first it seemed like any other conversation we had overheard. As it progressed, though, there was a dramatic crescendo until she was yelling at Ira rather than speaking to her. Her yelling unnerved me, but what was more troublesome was how, after finishing her tirade at Ira, she would turn toward us and smile.

"When we received the phone call from the NAC yesterday, we expected you to arrive," she yelled. "When you didn't show up yesterday afternoon, we thought that you had changed your mind."

She smiled sweetly at us as Ira translated.

"I thought we would have been here yesterday afternoon as well!" I replied with a smile, confused by the change in her attitude.

Nina Svetlanova laughed with us as Ira translated. Then she glared at Ira as she began to tell us about the three children who were available at the orphanage.

"We have a boy who is about to turn four. He has some problems with his skin, but is fine other than that. You may want to consider him. He is a sweet boy."

She smiled at us as Ira translated.

"We're interested in the little girl."

She turned to Ira, voice raised, glaring at her as she spoke.

"We also have a boy who is two, and he is about to become available for adoption. Then there is the girl. Of course, there are the special needs."

"We're interested in the girl."

89

"Well, you must really be open to special needs, if you are interested in the girl. She has many."

"Many?" We were confused.

"Yes, and we do not want you to meet her unless you are willing to really consider her, as a family rejected her just a few weeks ago ... she has no right arm, and her feet are clubbed."

We sat there, speechless, as we absorbed what she had just said.

The director and Ira spoke for several more minutes and then the director stepped out of the room.

Ira seemed shocked. "I am sorry that she is different than what they first said. They wanted to get you here to meet her and were afraid that the truth would scare you off. Now that you are here, they are willing to talk to you about the healthy boy. They think that since you now know the truth you won't want the little girl."

"We want to meet the girl. We came here to meet her." I said as my mind raced with thoughts. *They lied to us! I can't believe they lied to us about her disabilities ... blatantly lied ... not even a lie that they could cover up!*

The director returned and Ira told her what we said.

"Well," she replied, "you must understand that she is very very sick."

Sick? I thought, *sick with what? She is missing an arm, her feet are clubbed, she is sick ... hepatitis? HIV? cancer? The missing limbs are doable, but can we bring home a kid that is really sick?*

"What is she sick with?" I asked.

"She is missing her arm and her feet are clubbed," Ira replied.

"That's not sick," I said, "that's disabled. Does she have an illness?"

"No."

Relief flooded over me, although I was still wary of everything since they had lied to us about her disabilities. Could they be lying right now about her state of health? They lied to us once; I wouldn't put it past them to lie again.

"Then let's meet her," Rob said.

The director sent her secretary to fetch this little girl whom they called Halyna, and I watched the minute hand on the clock directly across from me. We waited for what seemed like an eternity but was really only a matter of minutes. The director filled the time with more information about the "darling little boy that we could meet if we decided that we did not want this little girl." Her speech about the boy was followed by a short speech about how we needed to be kind when we rejected the little girl.

"You must be kind in your reaction to her," Ira translated for the director. "We love her dearly and do not want you to hurt her feelings. We understand if you do not want her, but we must not let her understand that you are rejecting her."

It was obvious that she did not believe that we really wanted to adopt this girl, and she was almost convincing us that we shouldn't. As I waited for the secretary to retrieve Halyna, as they called her, I tried to figure out who was in on the lie. Ira was as shocked as we. That meant that it had to be either the director, the state psychologist at the NAC, or both.

In the end, I thought, *does it matter who lied about Halyna's disabilities? We are here to meet the child that had been hand-picked by Jesus for our family.*

"Halyna is ready to meet you," the secretary announced from the doorway, interrupting my thoughts.

We followed the secretary down the hallway to the other side of the building. It seemed as though we would never reach the room, and my stomach was all knotted up from the excitement of finally meeting my daughter. Ira, the director, one of the doctors, and several other workers followed us. It seemed as though the entire orphanage staff had an interest in Halyna's future, rooting for her to finally have a family.

We rounded the last corner and passed through a set of double doors that led to the waiting room. As soon as we stepped into the room, my eyes instantly rested upon the tiniest three-year-old I had ever seen. She was sitting on a little bench on the opposite side of the room. A red dress and a large red bow, which was tied in her cropped hair, contrasted with her fair skin, and brown eyes. Her right sleeve lay limp at her side. It was the first time I had ever seen a child amputee. She stared at us, wide-eyed, and scooted behind the arm of the caregiver that was sitting next to her. Everyone who knew her laughed at her shyness. I stood there, staring at her with tears in my eyes. Neither Rob nor I could fathom how someone could be so tiny. Later I learned that she was able to easily fit in clothing that was sized for an infant. She was so beautiful and so vulnerable that I could not stop myself from crying.

At her caregivers' bidding she hobbled over to me and gave me a hug. Then she hugged Rob. She was shocked by his beard, made a hilarious face as it scratched her cheek, and quickly retreated to her caregivers.

Her willingness to try to connect with us, despite her shyness, overwhelmed me. I sat there, right in the same spot where she had hugged me, and cried. Rob sat down next to her and smiled at her. Time seemed frozen for a couple minutes. No one spoke a word as we simply admired this little girl. Then I looked at Rob and he looked at me. We both knew.

"Yes?" I asked.

"Yes," he said.

"We want to adopt her," I told Ira.

"What? You know already? Are you sure? I mean you can think about it for a few days if you want."

"No," we both insisted, "this is our little girl. We want her."

Ira turned to the director and told her.

"*Da?*" she asked.

"*Da,*" Ira replied.

"*Da?*" she asked again.

"*Da!*" Ira said.

The director looked at us.

"*Da! Da!* Yes! Yes!" we said.

"Praise the Lord!" the director shouted as she jumped up to hug and kiss us.

Tears flowed, and there were hugs and kisses all around. Not understanding what was happening, Halyna just looked at us all, wide-eyed and surprised at the sudden outburst of joy.

A caregiver asked her, "Halyna, would you like this nice man and woman to be your Mama and Papa?"

Then *her* eyes widened with joy. Her face glowed, a smile broke out, and she whispered, *"Da."*

Again, there were cheers, tears, and hugs.

I pointed at myself and said, "Mama!"

She looked at me, walked over to where I sat on the floor, and sat down in my lap. Placing her hand on my face, she looked directly into my eyes and said two words that I will never forget.

"Muia Mama." My Mama.

Looking at Rob she smiled, but stayed in my lap — a bit gun-shy after her experience with his beard.

"Papa."

I held her in my lap, unable to do anything but cry as I observed what was happening: The culmination of two years of work and many years of prayer. God had been good to us and blessed us beyond what we could imagine. I had found my little girl. In an orphanage on the opposite side of the world, with the help of people I had never met before the plane touched down in Kyiv, I found my Anna Halyna, and she was as perfect as I had always dreamed her to be.

Some of the crowd in the room dissipated as people returned to their duties and others called their families to spread the news that Halyna had a family. We stayed with her for the next few minutes, just taking joy in the fact that we had finally found her. Suddenly I realized that she was asking me a question. I fumbled for words to respond though, because, of course, what she spoke was, as Rob calls it "Rus-Kranian" — a blend of the two related languages spoken throughout the country. Ira jumped in though, and translated, "She's asking you where her dress is."

"What dress is she talking about?"

"I'm not sure," Ira replied. "She's asking where you're keeping it and why you don't have it with you ... or if you have it hidden in your bag ... She wants to see it. I will have to ask the workers what she is talking about."

After a few minutes of discussion with the orphanage staff, Ira explained, "It is tradition here for a little girl to get a new dress when she goes home with her new parents. Halyna has seen many children go home with their families, and she has seen many beautiful dresses. She has been waiting and waiting for her Mama and Papa to come and bring a beautiful dress for her to wear home."

"We can't take you home today," I said, and Anna's face fell. Rob continued the explanation.

"We have to get permission from a judge before we can take you home. On Monday we will go see him, and then we will have to wait some days before he can give us permission. Then we will bring you your dress and take you home."

We did have a special dress for her, one that I had brought with us just for that day when we would take her home. It was a lavender dress, with a beautiful floral print all over it. It had a matching barrette and black patent leather shoes. I knew that Anna would love it.

"Well," Ira said, "since we are going to be here for a while, we need to find a place to stay."

As we were saying good-bye to Anna, a group of children burst into the room.

"Mama! Papa! Mama! Papa! Mama! Papa!"

The kids were everywhere, hugging us and calling us with smiling little faces. I tried to greet each one, looking at their hopeful little eyes. The girls wore dresses, tights, and hair bows just like Anna's. The two boys, the ones the director had tried to convince us to adopt, wore shirts and shorts with tights under them. Each one was beautiful, each one was begging for our attention. That is until a harsh voice cut through the din.

"*Nyet!* ... Halyna Mama *e* Papa!"

It was our timid, sweet Anna, and she was staking out her territory. She continued her little speech in Ukrainian, "This is *my* Mama and *my* Papa, and you must all stay away. I am going to go *home* with them. They are here to get permission from the judge for *me*. Stay back, they are *mine*."

To my utter amazement the children backed off. I quickly learned that although my daughter may be little, she wasn't afraid to defend her territory. We had our work cut out for us, and she would have much to learn about living in a family. I knew she would get a good amount of practice sharing our affection, as we were not going to ignore these children while we visited the orphanage.

But, that lesson would have to wait. It was time for us to go and find lodging. Once we were settled in we could visit her over the weekend and then officially start the adoption on Monday with a visit to the Regional Inspector.

Bureaucratic Snags

Bureaucracy is the art of making the possible impossible.
— Attributed to Javier Pascual Salcedo

If there is a way to delay important decisions, the good bureaucracy, public or private, will find it.
— Anonymous

Trust in the Lord with all your heart. Lean not on your own understanding. In all your ways acknowledge him and he will make your paths straight.
— Proverbs 3:4-5 (NIV)

Monday morning, exactly one week after our arrival in Ukraine, marked the official beginning of our adoption of Anna. Up to that point, we had been working toward *an* adoption, but it wasn't until we met with the Regional Inspector that the process for Anna's adoption could begin. We woke early and walked to the building that housed the Inspector. Although she had not even arrived for work, there was already a line of people waiting to meet with her.

We sat on a wooden bench outside her office, and Ira began talking to an elderly lady and a young boy.

"It is so difficult, sometimes," she told us.

Focused on the adoption, I responded, "I agree." Then a wave of guilt splashed over me, as I realized she was referring to her conversation with the lady.

"Her daughter has just died. That is her grandson. She is taking custody of him. His father is gone — disappeared a long time ago. She is here to register with the Inspector and, then, she hopes to receive a pension from the government to help with the cost of raising him."

"Is she entitled to anything?" I asked, looking back and forth at the elderly woman who did not look as though she was up to the task of raising a boy, and at the boy who looked sad, worried, and displaced.

"She is, but I don't know how much it will help. She will only get about $5 a month."

In addition to the grandmother and her grandson there was another couple ahead of us in line. Their reason for seeing the inspector: *propiska*, a draconian stamp that was placed into every citizen's internal passport. Left over from Soviet days, it designated the city or region that the owner of the passport may live. This couple wished to move, but couldn't do so without permission.

As we waited, my mind was distracted with thoughts about home. I couldn't help but compare my own situation with that of these few people sitting around me. It seemed impossible that $5 a month could really help anyone raise a child, and I certainly couldn't imagine having to obtain permission to move to a different part of my own country. Yet, when I was home I, more often than not, complained about our government, laws, and all the social services offered to our citizens. I began to realize that God might be using this trip for something more than just to increase the size of our family.

Before long, the Regional Inspector arrived. A petite, professionally dressed lady, with a CEO haircut and American-style glasses, the inspector was all business. She spoke a small amount of English, and, from what she communicated, it appeared she did not like us. The office was normally staffed with two inspectors. This week, however, one was on vacation, so that left us with an inspector who was overloaded with the work of two people. She did not seem to be overly concerned with the adoption of a couple from America.

From the start, the interview threw us for a loop. Until then, all the interviews had been perfunctory questions. She was the first official to see that she had all of our information and paperwork, so rather than asking the obvious, she jumped into the interview.

"You already have two children. Why do you want to have more?"

It was a simple question, one we should have been able to answer. But, neither of us expected it. We expected the typical, "Your names are Deborah and Robert Amend?" Or "You live in Ohio?" "You have completed all the necessary paperwork?"

This question required some thought ... we just wanted more children. Was there a good reason for that? Did she want some kind of deep psychological analysis of our childhoods? Did she want some type of deeply religious answer about God calling us here? What was she getting at? What could we say? I stammered. Rob kind of coughed. How could we explain why we wanted more than two kids? How could I understand the motivation behind my desire to have a big family? The impatient inspector was visibly irritated with us and reiterated the question several times through Ira. Then she even switched to English.

"Why? Why? Why more kids? You have two already! Why?"

Finally, I managed to say, "We just want a big family."

"Good."

That was it. I thought to myself. *Couldn't she just have realized we wanted a big family?*

She and Ira continued to talk. Unable to follow the Ukrainian conversation, my mind wandered, relieved that the unexpected interview seemed to be over. Then Ira delivered the big blow.

"The adoption has to be approved by a guardianship council before we can apply for a court date. The council does not meet until the last Thursday of the month, May 30. We can do nothing else with the adoption until then."

May 30 was over two weeks away. I started to feel dizzy. This part of the process was only supposed to take up a couple days, and here it was a week after we had arrived and we were being told that we would have to wait for two more weeks to simply start the process.

"We have to get home ... we have children at home, jobs to get back to...."

The inspector just looked at us over the top of her glasses.

"Oh, you will make arrangements, then. This cannot be changed. The council *must* approve this before you can apply for court. I have no power to change that law."

Tears were burning in my eyes as we left. I could not believe that this could be happening. In my mind rang the words from Proverbs:

> *Trust in the Lord with all your heart, lean not on your*
> *own understanding; in all your ways acknowledge him,*
> *and he will make your paths straight.*
> — Proverbs 3:5-6 (NIV)

Those words could have been a comfort, but I would not let them. The very thing that I did not want to deal with was happening. God was requiring of me the one thing that I was not willing to give him, the one string that I had kept attached to this adoption. God was trying to use this adoption to do more than grow the size of our family and, at that point in time, I became very aware of it. And I was angry. In anger, I prayed that God would keep his promise to make the path straight.

Make my path straight God, I prayed, *do what you promised. Expedite this adoption!*

As we headed to the orphanage for a visit, Ira phoned the NAC to find out more about this law.

"It's a regional law. Only three regions in Ukraine have the law, and the NAC is powerless to change it," she told us, after she had hung up her phone. She was as frustrated as we were with the situation.

"Did they offer any help at all?" I asked, at this point firmly believing that all Ukrainians must have the misunderstanding that Americans are all independently wealthy and able to be away from home for months at a time.

"The psychologist suggested we try appealing to the mayor of Vinnitsa. Since it is a regional law, the NAC can't override it."

As we rode along in the city bus taking us to the orphanage, I considered our options. My heart was, once again, broken at the thought of being away from my boys for so long. The thought of two weeks was bad enough, but now we were facing an indefinite stay in Ukraine. What would this do to their mental health? Would they feel like we had abandoned them? What about my parents? How long could we expect them to put their lives on hold and care for Ben and Justin? I was so homesick for my boys I could hardly keep back the tears.

Maybe we should just throw in the towel, I thought to myself. It was the first time that I had ever considered giving up on the adoption. We had come this far, had actually met Anna, but I felt completely defeated.

The bus dropped us off at the top of the street, and we began to walk the rest of the way to the orphanage. The street was falling apart and had huge potholes all over it. It ran past the back of some houses that had not survived the effects of time and poverty very well. However, they often had pretty gardens in the back, both vegetable and flower. The street itself was lined with cherry trees. On that early spring day, the leaves were just starting to bud. Chickens, of various types, ran all over the street, accompanied by a unique bird the locals referred to as a "turk-duck," a cross between a turkey and a duck. The striking beauty of Ukrainian nature, juxtaposed to the dilapidated buildings was another aspect of Ukrainian life that fascinated me.

As I took in the sights of neighborhood, though, I just couldn't shake the depression that I was feeling.

Could we just walk away? What about Anna? Would it matter to her? I pondered these thoughts as we approached the orphanage. *We just met her a couple days before, and we hardly knew her.*

After all, hasn't she known nothing but life in an institution? Would she even know what she was missing?

Then I heard something that answered my question: "Mama! Mama! Mama! Mama!"

A child was yelling "Mama" so loudly that we heard her long before we entered the orphanage. Rob and I raised our eyebrows at each other as if to question the sanity of the child that was yelling. As we walked toward Anna's room, the yelling grew louder. We knocked, the door was opened, and we stepped in.

There was Anna hobbling toward us as fast as she could, away from her spot at the window where she had stood waiting for us, yelling, "Mama, Mama, Mama!"

She jumped up into my arms and gave me a big kiss and a hug. Then cautiously avoiding the beard, she hugged Rob.

The rest of the morning was so busy that I did not even have time to think about how badly the adoption process was going. Her group was bundling up for a walk when we arrived, and we were invited to go along.

I offered to help Anna get ready. One of the caregivers handed me the clothing that she needed. It was an unusually warm spring day in Vinnitsa, and in my pants and short-sleeved shirt, I was quite comfortable. I was a bit confused about all the clothing I was handed. After all, Anna was already dressed.

"What do I do with this...?" I tentatively asked Ira. She just looked at me like maybe I needed to get over my jet lag.

"You dress Anna with it," she replied.

"Should I take off the other clothes first?"

"No, just layer it on."

So, over the T-shirt, underwear, dress, and tights that she was already wearing, I put on another pair of tights, a heavy sweater, a coat, and a woolen cap. Then, I placed boots on her feet. Now, apparently, she was all ready for a nice spring walk.

There was a stroller for Anna, but she preferred to walk, hobbling behind her group. I am not sure if she simply preferred to walk, or if she chose walking in order to protect her territory. Every time one of the children tried to talk to us, they were stopped with a sharp word from her, "Back off ... they're *mine*."

102

We spent the rest of the morning playing with her and, to her dismay, the rest of her group as well. We looked at the budding trees, checked on the vegetable garden, and studied a nest of ants near the edge of one path. We discovered that she (and the rest of the children) loved books. And, we discovered that we could not give up on this adoption. This was our little girl, just as much as Ben and Justin were our little boys. To leave her would be to abandon our own.

As the day progressed, I began to place my trust, not in the Lord, but in the mayor. I was certain that he could be the ticket to our expedited adoption. The mayor of Vinnitsa had been recently elected. He was very popular (his picture hung on the wall in the orphanage director's office), and everyone kept telling us that he was very "young" and "progressive." We hoped that would mean that he was reasonable.

The next morning we awoke, early again, so as to avoid those lines, and went with Ira to try to talk to the mayor.

This government building was more modern than the others we had been in. It looked to have been built in the late '60s or early '70s. A woman sold baked goods, women's clothing, and fur coats in the lobby. The hallways were in disrepair, with missing lights, dirty walls, and the occasional missing window. However, when we stepped into the mayor's office, it all changed. Hardwood floors, wood paneling on the walls, and ceiling-to-floor bookcases created the décor of the secretaries' office. Two secretaries sat at large desks on either side of the room, and on those desks were something I had not seen in any other government office: computers.

Ira spoke to the secretaries, and we learned that all of our hopes had been in vain. It did not matter how progressive the mayor was because he was out of town. His vice-mayor, though, was working in his stead for the time being. She directed us to his office down the hall.

The vice-mayor, however, was not young and progressive, but middle-aged and grumpy. We waited for an hour outside his office, as he did not believe that he should make the time to meet with some adoptive couple from America. When it was finally our turn, Ira felt it best that she talk to him and we wait in the hallway, so we nervously waited outside the closed door. The final answer came shortly.

He told her, in essence, that when Americans come to Ukraine to adopt, they should expect to follow all the laws. They should not expect special treatment. They should plan on spending a significant amount of time in Ukraine. After all, their children are precious and the adoption laws are there to protect them.

That was well and good, but what he really meant was: The guardianship council was comprised of over twenty members, all of whom must put their stamp of approval on the papers in order to apply for the court date. There was no way to rearrange the meeting for an earlier date, as so many people were involved. We would simply have to wait until May 30.

I was devastated. We went back to the hotel and phoned home to share the terrible news. My father answered the phone, and I abashedly updated him about the situation, realizing the implications it held for him. He was not surprised and assured us that they could care for the boys while we waited until May 30.

Then he put Ben on the line. "Hi, Mom!" His voice was so little and sweet — and sounded so far away.

"Hi, sweetie! How are you?"

"Are you still in Ukraine?"

"Yes." *And will be for quite some time*, I thought.

"Then why are you speaking English?" he asked, completely baffled.

"Because I don't know how to speak Ukrainian," I answered.

"Yes, but you told me that all the people in Ukraine speak Ukrainian, so since you are in Ukraine, you should be speaking Ukrainian."

"If it were only that easy ... Hey! It looks like Daddy and I are going to be stuck here for a while. Anna is fine, but the government has decided that they need to take a long time to let us bring her home. I am really sorry, I...." Tears filled my eyes as I began to apologize for destroying his mental health by abandoning him for so long.

"More time! Wow! That would mean more candy! Did you know that Grandpa keeps candy in his pocket and snack cakes under his seat in his car? Grandma has made us pancakes and oatmeal every day this week. And Grandpa couldn't find the video that needed to go back to the library, so he promised a trip to the toy store for whoever found it. Justin found it in less than one minute. He got some dinosaur Legos ... Grandpa also bought us ice cream and...."

I handed the phone to Rob. It broke my heart to hear anymore. As Ben, and then Justin, chatted away to their dad about the great life they were leading back in the USA, I lay on the bed and sobbed. My heart was completely torn with the pain of missing them, and the fear that, all of a sudden, they would crash into a terrible depression over missing us.

It just can't be good for them to be separated from us like this, I thought.

"What are you trying to do to them, God?" I prayed, "Destroy them? Kill their faith? Make them suffer for our choice to obey you?"

I raged at God for putting us in this situation. I raged at him for not answering our prayers the way that we had wanted them answered. We had stepped out in faith and it had been difficult. But this, this was beyond difficult. I was fully aware that we could be stuck in Ukraine working on this adoption for ages. The judge could take as long as he wanted to set the court date. Then there was the thirty-day waiting period. Then there was at least a week's worth of work after that to complete her immigration. At that time, I completely understood that I was going to be in Ukraine for at least one month and probably longer.

"You promised to make my path straight!" I sobbed to him, as though he had broken a promise.

Using that passage of scripture, I bombarded God with my anger about him not making this path the path that I wanted to walk. I wanted him to make the path straight by making it easy and by removing the burdens. I wanted obedience to God's calling to be easy (after all, this was something we had volunteered to do); it felt like he should make it that way. I wanted it to contain only the sacrifices that we had been willing to make. But, instead of changing the path we were on, he chose to help us travel it. As I raged at

God for not bailing us out, I realized that Ben and Justin were fine. They were not experiencing any of the angst that I was. They simply waited, in joyful and candy-filled anticipation, for the arrival of their sister. They did not worry that we would not come home, they had complete faith that God would do what he promised he would do.

What God wanted, though, was to teach me to trust him. Sitting in that hotel room in Vinnitsa, Ukraine, thousands of miles from my children, I had no choice but to trust in the goodness of God. I had to trust that he would establish his own relationship with Ben and Justin, he would meet their emotional needs, and he would protect them. I had to trust that he loved them even more than I did. I had to be willing to give up that one thing that I had been unwilling to give to him: my children.

It was a battle that raged inside me the entire time I was in Ukraine. There were times when I won and there were times when my thoughts would drift in the wrong direction and I would harden my heart. However, as with so much of the adoption, we had no choice but to move on. So, we dug in our heels, and set up to wait until the guardianship council met.

The Baby House

A baby is God's opinion that life should go on.
— Carl Sandberg

The biggest disease today is not leprosy or tuberculo-sis, but rather the feeling of being unwanted.
— Mother Teresa of Calcutta

So it is not the will of your Father who is in heaven that one of these little ones perish.
— Matthew 18:14 (NIV)

In all of Europe, we could not have found better company than the ten children that formed Anna's *groupa*.

The Baby House was organized like most orphanages in the former Soviet Union. Most of the children entered the orphanage as infants and remained there until they were four or five years old. The children were housed in various sections of the orphanage, organized by age into groups. The infants were kept separate from the older children, which meant that siblings were often separated.

Such was the case of one little girl in Anna's *groupa*. Her name was Karina.

Karina and her younger sister entered the orphanage not long before we arrived. The hope was that it would be a temporary stay until her mother could find a job. With no father around to help, the family had fallen into such poverty that she could no longer provide even basic necessities for her children. Karina was a beautiful girl with thick, long, black hair, not cropped short like Anna's since she was not a permanent placement in the orphanage. Every day the caregivers would brush her hair and weave it into two braids that were tied with bright red bows. Her beautiful hair, coupled with a bright, cheerful dress created the picture of a beautiful girl — with the saddest eyes I have ever seen.

In all our time in Ukraine, I never once saw Karina with dry eyes. The first time we saw her she was trailing behind the other children, crying.

"Can we adopt her, too?" Rob asked me, only half joking. The sadness that surrounded her was almost like a cloud.

"Why is she crying?" I asked a caregiver.

"She misses her baby sister. We try to take Karina to see her at least once a day, but it is not always possible. She has not seen her in two days and will not today. Her sister's group is quarantined because a couple of the infants are sick. We cannot risk spreading the sickness through Karina."

Another child in Anna's *groupa* was a temporary placement. Natasha had strawberry blond hair, blue eyes, and pudgy cheeks. Some days she would be cheerful, but most days she was sad. Whenever we arrived, she would shyly take my hand (whenever Anna wasn't looking) and whisper to me, "I miss my Mama."

One day, though, was different.

"Halyna Mama Papa!" she called to us when we arrived at the orphanage. Her eyes were glowing with excitement.

"Muia Mama!" Her Mama had come to visit her. She hugged her Mama's knees as she introduced us. That day, she was the happiest child in the orphanage, and several days later, she went home.

There was also little Lena. Pudgy cheeks, olive skin, brown eyes, and black hair. She never spoke a word, but from the moment we would arrive, she would walk up to Rob and grab his hand, with no plans to let go.

Anna's best friends were Luba, Tonya, and Andrushka. Luba was a little girl who had been with Anna since their first days at the orphanage. Anna was very devoted to her. She looked a lot like Anna, with short, dark blonde hair and brown eyes. However, that was where the similarities ended. Luba was very quiet and shy.

Tonya was four years old, with large brown eyes and brown hair. She reminded me of a baby doll, with her round face and eyes that often held a vacant stare. For reasons we didn't completely understand, Tonya was not available for adoption. Her mother was an alcoholic, and none of her birth family was able to care for her, yet their rights to parent her had not been terminated. So, she stayed at the orphanage with no hope for a future. Before long, she would be headed to the next phase of orphanage life: boarding school.

In the best possible situation, the children who were not adopted from the Baby House were moved onto a boarding school. There they would live and be educated, and, theoretically prepared for life. Like orphanages, each boarding school varies greatly. In the worst case scenario, neglect and abuse rule the school. In the best scenarios, the children are nurtured and educated, even possibly aimed toward higher education. However, for the most part, orphanage boarding schools hold no esteem with the general public. The "diploma" from such a school does not advance the child. In fact, in many circumstances, it creates quite the opposite effect, and it is a stigma difficult to overcome.

At age fifteen or sixteen they graduate from the system unprepared for life, with no familial support and no specific credentials. According to the World Orphan Project, nearly 10% of them will commit suicide before turning eighteen. Approximately 60% of the girls turn to prostitution, but the industry targets those girls because they are alone and vulnerable. The statistics show that 70% of the boys turn to crime, and most of those will die from violence or from contracting tuberculosis in prisons.[1]

Then there is the worst possible situation, most likely the one that Tonya faced, for Tonya was born with fetal alcohol syndrome. FAS and its sister condition, Fetal Alcohol Effect, FAE (a milder form of the same problem), are chronic problems in many former Soviet Union countries. And, in Tonya's case, it took the form of a language problem and behavior problems. At four years of age, she could still not speak in a tangible way. Her developmental disabilities would soon be assessed, and she would move on to a different type of children's home — one for the disabled.

In Russian boarding schools for older, healthy orphans are called *internats*. Homes for the *imbetsil* "imbecile" children, which are children who are deemed uneducable, are called *pyschoneurological internats*. According to Human Rights Watch, a 1996 report from Ukraine showed that approximately 30% of all disabled children who lived in one of these homes died before reaching the age of eighteen.[2] Throughout former Soviet Union countries, children in these homes face malnourishment, severe neglect, and a lifetime of abuse. I had seen photos of disabled children locked in completely dark rooms, tied to benches and chairs, and forced to lie in bed. These photos, released by several human rights groups, all flashed through my mind as I pondered Tonya's future.

Every time she would run past me, wildly shouting her garbled words, or grab my leg to hug me, a piece of my heart would break as I thought about how her future would not be redeemed. And, it did not help that Anna loved Tonya. Though often out of control, and even violent at times, Tonya was Anna's friend, and when Anna loves someone, she is committed to them.

Andrushka was the little boy the director thought we might want to adopt. He was bright, curious, affectionate, and excited about everything. His big, dark eyes always had a spark in them, and his face grinned so much I wondered how his cheeks didn't hurt. He always wore a shirt, shorts, and tights — a clothing ensemble for which I was never able to uncover the reasons. Every time I asked if he wore shorts and tights out of necessity or tradition, I never heard a straight answer.

"Mama and Papa!" he greeted us every day with a big grin. We loved to talk with him because he never understood that we spoke a different language than he. So, he was always trying to correct the words that we used.

"We brought you milk," I told him one day. "Milk."

He looked at me very seriously when he responded, *"Nyet Milk ... Molokoh."* — no milk. For all the joy that he exhibited, Andrushka's heart, too, was filled with sadness.

"You know," a caregiver told us one day, "Andrushka cries himself to sleep every night."

"Why?" I asked.

"Because he wants a Mama and a Papa. Every day he asks us, 'Today will my Mama and Papa come?' And every night he cries himself to sleep because the answer is still, 'No.' "

There was a boy, though Anna did not know him well, who completely captured my heart. His name was Edik. He was the youngest in the group and always getting into trouble. We often heard the adults crying out to or about him as the children played.

"Oi! Edik!" Someone would cry. Then would follow a little boy being taken into a separate room for a spanking, a change of clothing, or some bandaging — depending upon what he had done. He constantly wet his pants, ate dirt, and pulled things apart. He was an adorable little boy.

One day, we were sitting in the foyer reading books to Anna. Ira was not with us, so our communication was limited. After looking at several books, Anna stood up and started to walk around the room. She ran her hand up and down the walls as she walked and then stopped at a place where a small piece of wall paper had been ripped off. Furrowing her little eyebrows, she looked at us, pointed at the wallpaper and said one word, "Edik."

There were others in the *groupa* as well, and each time we visited, we tried to give them as much attention as we could. The children did not know what to make of us, as we not only talked funny, but looked funny (especially Rob, as men are very novel to children in orphanages) as well.

One day, upon our arrival, the children ran to greet us. Karina, always teary-eyed, would not take her eyes off of Rob's face. Most of the children had no idea what to make of his beard, so I figured that she was studying it. However, on that day, she was set on more than looking. She slowly walked toward Rob, with her right arm raised and her index finger extended.

Rob glanced sideways at me, smiled, and said, "This is going to be interesting...."

She continued her walk forward, finger raised, and with great concentration on her face, walked right up to Rob's face. Ten pairs of little eyes followed her, while a rush of whispers created an environment of suspense. Then, ever so gently, she wiggled his glasses up and down. All the children sighed with relief as she ran away. They had never seen glasses before and had thought that they were part of his face.

To the children at the Baby House, we were walking enigmas.

Anna, clearly, was the kingpin. Her physical condition mandated little movement, so Andrushka, a bubbly fountain of energy, worked as her henchman. I was always amazed at how the rest of the children would, literally, obey Anna's commands. She was little, but feisty.

Whenever we visited, she always wanted to play with us in view of the children, showing off the fact that she now had parents. Second to showing off, she liked to play on the playgrounds that belonged to the other groups. Generally, those playgrounds were *verboten* to her, as they liked to keep the groups separate in order to control the germ pool. However, if we were watching her, Anna was allowed to move about the outside grounds of the orphanage as we pleased. We spent much of our time exploring the various playgrounds.

Rob would jokingly refer to the playgrounds as the "Tetanus Playgrounds." At one time, they were probably wonderful. However, time and poverty had worked their effect on them and they were in terrible disrepair. Grass grew up all around them, and each piece of equipment had at least one part missing. The bench swing, which was Anna's favorite, was missing part of its seat back. The slide appeared old and rusty. Upon further inspection, though, I realized that it was actually made of splintering wood. I learned, quickly and painfully, to always look before I sat. Nails stuck up out of the wood in places where they had worked loose.

However, the children loved to play outside. And, having never seen a safety-inspected playground like American children are spoiled with, the children were pleased with what was there. Compared to what many other orphanages had to offer, these playgrounds were truly a blessing. I was constantly amazed at how the caregivers were able to find stimulating play for the children, when it seemed as though there were so few objects with which they could play.

Another group had a playground around the corner of the building from Anna's. That playground held her favorite toy on all the orphanage grounds — a large toy car.

"Mashina! Mashina!" She would say when we would walk past it. She loved to stop at the car and pretend to drive it. Having never been in an actual car, this little toy one was very exciting.

Even more than visiting other playgrounds, she loved to play with us near her *groupa*. In addition to showing off her new parents, Anna could then keep tabs on what the other children were doing. She was always certain that she would not miss out on anything. Often our time was spent with all ten children, all of whom we found very entertaining.

"These are books," Rob told a group of five or six children, one day.

"Nyet," Andrushka looked truly sympathetic as he corrected Rob. *"Knieshka."*

"Yes," Rob replied, *"knieshka* ... books."

"Hmm," Andrushka and Anna looked at each other with great mercy in their eyes.

"Your poor Papa," Andrushka said, in Ukrainian, "he does not even know the proper word for book."

"Yes," Anna replied, certain that the beard was some type of disfigurement that she would just have to accept and love, "and he has a beard. Poor Papa, but I love my Papa even though he does have a beard...."

Rob continued to look at books with the children, each child grabbing whichever book they could get their hands on. They were adorable as they ate up the attention from us and as they enjoyed looking at books. At least, I thought so. Anna, on the other hand, had a different opinion.

"Back off ... these are my Papa's books. I have a Papa, and these are his books," she proclaimed loudly. "Since he is my Papa and these are his books, they are my books. Do not touch."

113

Trying to explain the concept of sharing, Rob took our Ukrainian-English dictionary from one of the children and looked up the word "share."

"*Dolia!*" he said, triumphantly, hoping he had found the correct Ukrainian word for "share."

Anna's face fell.

Every other child's face brightened and peace reigned for the next few minutes.

We would look at books with them, walk with them, and push them on the bench swing. I enjoyed the times at the bench swing, as I was able to talk to her caregivers as I pushed her and several friends. Through them, including one lady who had cared for her as an infant, I was able to piece together parts of Anna's story.

Anna entered the orphanage as an infant, straight from the hospital. There she was received by women who not only cared for her, but prayed for her. Knowing what her future would be if she remained an orphan, they prayed for God to send a family for her — one from the United States, where they felt she would get the best medical care possible. They told her, and the other children, that God did have a family for her, and that her Mama and Papa would one day fly to Ukraine on an airplane and come to get her. Whenever an airplane would fly over the children would jump up and point at it, "A plane! Maybe this one will bring a Mama and Papa!"

That is how an airplane became a sign of hope for Anna, and, as a result, a reminder of God's provision for me. As I pieced together the story of Anna's history at the orphanage, I realized an amazing thing. Between our family and her caregivers, someone had been praying for Anna, every day of her life, since the day she entered the orphanage. Not only was Anna the answer to our prayers, but we were the answer to the prayers of the ones who first loved her.

And love her they did, as these ladies went far beyond the call of duty. Often, they never even received pay for their work (if the government has no money, then there is no money to pay government employees). They faithfully cared for each of the children. Food was made from scratch, clothing hand washed, gardens tended, and floors scrubbed. Beyond that, they built in her a strong sense of her heritage, with Easter celebrations, visits from Grandfather Frost at Christmas, retelling and acting out folk tales, and singing and dancing. I am firmly convinced that Anna received a much richer cultural education in her years at the Baby House than many American children receive sitting in front of cable television in their large, suburban homes.

In fact, even her transition from the infant group to the pre-school group was treated with great love.

"Halyna is so loving," an infant caregiver told me. "She was so attached to us that her transition to the next group was difficult. Every night I would have to go over to her group and tuck her into bed because she missed us so much."

It was music to my ears. First, that her caregivers cared so much, and second that she was able to attach. If a child is able to attach to a caregiver in an orphanage, then they will be able to transfer that attachment to their parents. The love and care of the ladies of the Baby House laid the foundation for the success of Anna's entire life.

God's economy is the never the same as the world's. Books, television, and all the experts pander many products and experiences that they say our children "need." My time in Ukraine taught me that all of a child's needs can be met in a place where there is no money.

One time, we decided to pull Anna from the group to take a walk with her. Ira came with us, as Anna was essentially not trying to learn English. The second day we spent with her she spoke her first English word: book. She would repeat other words and try her best to communicate with us, until she figured out that Ira could translate for her. Then, she was perfectly happy to run every one of our communications through Ira. We were frustrated, but realized that she was not going to really learn English until we got her home and immersed her in the language.

So, that day, the four of us took a walk. She was a bit upset about it because she had planned to spend the morning showing us off to the other kids. Along the way she picked up a big stick, and started to sweep it across the path. "It is my broom," she announced.

We continued to walk with her sweeping her "broom" across the path. The more we walked, though, the wider she swept and the more it became apparent that she was trying to test our limits with the stick. Quickly, I thought of a non-confrontational solution. I snapped the end of the stick off so it was not quite so long. Then she could easily swing it and not hit anybody.

"Hmmp," she said as she looked at the end. "Well, my Mama tried to ruin it, but that is okay."

Obviously, she was a little miffed. She stopped near a branch of a path that led to another group's playground. The group was currently playing on it, which meant that we could not visit it — a fact that Anna was aware of. The orphanage kept strict quarantine rules in order to keep the kids healthy, and we had been told that this particular group was currently quarantined.

"We now go this way," she stated as she headed toward the playground. There was a tiny smile on her face.

We stopped her and reminded her about the rule.

"Hmmp ... then I will sweep." And with that she began to really wave that stick back and forth aiming directly for our knees.

I grabbed the stick and broke the top half off, leaving a stick that was, for all intents and purposes, too short to pretend it was a broom.

"Well," she said with a glint in her eye, "now it is no longer a broom. But it is the perfect stick for spanking Tonya. I will keep it for when I need to spank Tonya." And, she headed on down the path.

In one fell swoop, Rob picked her up, took the stick, and tossed it into the grass. "No," he said quietly. Then he gently set her down, and took her hand as she walked.

She looked at us, and, for the first time, realized that she was not going to always get her way. I looked at her, and for the first time, realized the strength of the personality that I was going to be raising. It was not the first time that her personality had shown through.

On our second or third visit I brought some clothing with me to see what would fit Anna. We found a quiet, private room for the four of us (Rob, Ira, Anna, and me), as the caregivers were very concerned that the other children not see all that Anna was getting. They knew it would break their hearts.

I opened the bag and pulled out the clothes. Anna noted the lack of a dress. I was careful not to bring one, as I did not want to send her the wrong message.

I held up the outfit I brought. Anna smiled as she looked at it, and I helped her undress. The layers of clothing were wet with sweat, and none of it smelled too pleasant. The dress and tights came off, and then she took off the underwear. I was glad she did not need help, as it was old and very dirty.

As she was undressing, it was the first time that Rob and I really got a good look at her legs. We had figured out the first time we met her that her feet were not clubbed. We took their usage of "clubbed feet" to mean that something was wrong with her feet. Something they believed could be corrected.

Looking at her legs that day, it became apparent that the real problem was that her legs were two different lengths, with her right foot even with her left knee. Then I noticed the toes. I had to count them twice, as I thought that my mind was playing tricks on me.

Before I could say anything, though, Rob made the observation. "Hey! She only has four toes on each foot."

"How about that," I said, "it's not every day you meet someone with four toes!"

We smiled at each other, thinking that, in light of everything else that was missing, a couple missing toes was not a big deal.

She finished dressing herself and smiled at us. "Now," she said, "we can take a walk in front of the other children."

"Anna Halyna," I said, "you can't wear the clothes anywhere ... we just brought them for you to try on."

"I want to wear them outside."

"You can't," Ira chimed in, "what if you fall down and get them dirty?"

"I will walk," she replied, "and I will not fall." She nodded her head once and looked at us as if to dare us to try to take the clothes away.

"Anna Halyna," I said, "you are going to have to take the clothes off. You can have them when it is time to go home!"

With the pronouncement of the magic word, "home," Anna obeyed. That word was like water to a thirsty, little soul, and whenever we brought it up, she did whatever we said. She had her own thoughts about what she wanted to do, but, more than anything, she wanted to go home.

After redressing she sat in my lap and laid her head on my shoulder. "I am tired of waiting ... I want to go home."

"As soon as the judge says we can...."

---

1. www.worldorphanproject.com.

2. Jo Becker, *Easy Targets Violence Against Children Worldwide* (New York: Human Rights Watch, 1996), p. 8.

Vinnitsa In Spring

I grew up in a typical Ukrainian village ... and it was beautiful. Green hills rose in the south behind the river, and the rich tar-black soil of the plains stretched to the north. The plains were divided into strips of fields. Every spring and summer these strips would disappear beneath miles of wheat. Waves of rich grain, green in spring and golden in summer, gently rolled in the summer breeze. — Miron Dolot
Execution by Hunger: The Hidden Holocaust

A traveler without observation is like a bird without wings. — Moslin Eddin Saadi

Then God said, "Let the land produce vegetation: seed-bearing plants and trees on the land that bear fruit with seed in it, according to their various kinds." And it was so. The land produced vegetation: plants bearing seed according to their kinds and trees bearing fruit with seed in it according to their kinds. And God saw that it was good. — Genesis 1:11-12 (NIV)

Streams of rainwater flowed around my ankles and collected into even deeper pools in the large potholes in and around the sidewalk. It had been raining most of the day, and every part of me felt soaked. My feet were drenched by the nearly inch-deep rain on the sidewalk, my back and clothes were drenched from rain blown in the wind.

Nothing seems to happen in moderation here, I thought to myself as we headed toward the local McDonald's. We had braved the rain for dinner because we needed to stay occupied. Even with all the time we spent at the Baby House, there was always much time left in each day. Not known as a big tourist region, we had quickly done all the sightseeing there was to be done, and it was when we were not occupied that we felt the most homesick. Walking seven blocks in the rain in order to spend an evening at McDonald's seemed a reasonable activity.

We had been in Ukraine for a couple weeks and were still over a week away from the meeting of the guardianship council. The rain was just one more thing to add to my sullen mood. Filling time was the number one problem we were having. We had long since read through all the reading material we brought and had even journeyed to the University of Vinnitsa bookstore (shelves and stands set up in a lobby of the University) to look for English literature. I had memorized the order of programming on the BBC, the only English-speaking television station our hotel television received and had become quite proficient at spades and hearts. We were so desperate, in fact, that we had come to the point where we were watching Ukrainian television.

The night before we had spent the evening watching *Who Wants to Be a Millionaire*. Though it was in Ukrainian, watching the show made me feel more connected to home. As I lay on my bed watching the television, I pondered the fact that one million *hryvnia* was nowhere near what the show was paying out to the Americans who won. It just didn't seem fair.

The 32,000-*hryvnia* question came up on the screen, and we picked out enough words to understand that they were asking the type of government used in Latvia.

We stared at the ABCD answers. The options appeared to be:

A. Presidential

B. Dictatorship

C. Parliamentary

D. Democratic

"What do you think?" I asked Rob.

"I would guess that it's C. It seems like most of Europe likes those parliamentary governments...."

"That's what I would answer, too," I said, lying down on the bed, my head almost hurting from all the translating.

There was debating and talking on the television and then the answer C highlighted. We were right!

"Hey!" I said, "we answered a game show question that was in Ukrainian! We could've earned 32,000 *hryvnia*. What do you think, honey?"

"I think that we've been here too long."

And, it had been so long. It wasn't that I didn't like the country of Ukraine. It wasn't that I didn't enjoy the beauty of the blossoming cherry and chestnut trees or the beautiful flowers with their vibrant colors. It wasn't that the lines and curves of the Cyrillic letters no longer fascinated me, nor that I didn't feel welcome by the church in Kyiv, or the ladies who cared for Anna. It wasn't the uncomfortable living conditions or even the lack of English. I missed my children at home. My heart was torn and placed in two places: Cincinnati, Ohio, and Vinnitsa, Ukraine, and until it was all back together again, I would not feel any real peace.

Lord, I prayed as we shook out our umbrellas and stepped into the McDonald's, *we need something to distract us, something to encourage us.*

The restaurant was crowded that night (McDonald's is a very hip place to eat in Ukraine!), and it took us several minutes to inch our way toward the counter. As we got in line behind a boy, we began to discuss our order with Ira. Suddenly, we were interrupted by a very American voice.

"Do you know how to order french fries in Russian?" It was the boy standing in line in front of us.

"You're American," both Rob and I gasped in astonishment!

"Ya. My mom and dad are kind of missionaries here. My dad's over there."

He pointed toward a man who was sitting in a booth with several children. Obviously not Ukrainian (he was wearing a plaid flannel shirt and had a beard), he smiled and waved at us. After ordering our food we went over and joined him at his table.

"You're American!" I said, stating the obvious.

"Yes," he said. Introducing himself, he continued, "We, my wife, children, and I, live here, as sort of unofficial missionaries. Officially, I am a songwriter, not a missionary."

We introduced ourselves to him. "We're here to adopt." Rob told him, and I related to him the saga of Anna's adoption. Through the conversation, I began to piece together that this man was a somewhat successful songwriter — having written songs for many famous Christian singers. Not only had we found another American, but one that was sort of a ... *celebrity*.

"One question," I said, as we were getting ready to leave. "How in the world did you end up living in Vinnitsa, Ukraine?"

"Well, back before the Soviet Union broke up, I wrote a song about the people in the Soviet Union — those people who were supposed to be my enemies. I was playing with my son in a park, and I thought about how there had to be fathers here playing with their sons in a park and that they couldn't be an enemy ... the Soviet Union fell, and I knew that I could write songs from here as easily as from the US. So, we prayed about it and God led us here."

Homesick and disgruntled from our interactions with the government officials, this family was truly a gift from God. Several days later we visited their home. A large home, it was up to western standards and included a basketball hoop, satellite TV, and an extensive (and mysteriously current) DVD collection. It was a well-timed respite for two very homesick Americans.

"An email from home!" I told Rob.

He was sitting at his computer and I was at mine. We were in a small internet café across the street from our hotel. A truly hip place to be, there were posters of American movies with Russian titles hanging on the walls, and we were surrounded by teenage boys playing computer games. However, Rob and I visited daily, communicating with those back home. The connection was painfully slow, often taking five minutes to download one email.

"If you come in the morning," the young manager told me, "the satellite is overhead and the signal is stronger. The internet is faster."

The phone lines all over the country were so archaic that this clever café owner just skipped the landlines and bought satellite hook up. It was a trend we saw all over Ukraine — skipping almost a generation of technology and going completely wireless since the infrastructure was so old.

So, the satellite for the internet café shaped our daily schedule. We breakfasted, went to visit Anna, and then headed over to the internet café. After our visit there, we ate lunch, relaxed at the hotel (read a book or watched the BBC on the little television in our room), and then went back to Anna's. After that visit, we did a little shopping and got dinner at one of three places: McDonald's, a local pizza place, or a small Ukrainian restaurant near the hotel.

The pizza place and the McDonald's almost could have been transplanted from America. The Ukrainian restaurant, though, had a lot of charm. The wooden booths were draped in silk ivy, and the waitresses wore traditional Ukrainian garb. Since we didn't want Ira to have to translate the entire menu every time we went there, we would ask for a recommendation. Often times it worked well, other times, we were not too sure.

"What is this?" I asked, pointing to an item on the menu. It appeared to be the special for the day.

"It is meat," Ira replied.

"What kind of meat?" I asked.

"It is ... meat ... I don't know ... meat."

At first, I thought that perhaps she didn't know the exact translation for the meat. However, after visiting several restaurants with various translators, not to mention visits to other former Soviet Union countries, we came to realize that it was simply meat with no identity. It had no animal tied to it, nor would anyone fess up to what part of an animal it came from. Maybe it was simply Russian SPAM™, but whatever the case, it took six more trips to Ukraine before we got the nerve to try it.

Cultural differences aside, we loved the beauty of Vinnitsa. Situated on both sides of the Bugh River, Vinnitsa is a large city filled with the hustle and bustle of the people, and the quiet reflections of churches, parks, several universities, and a prominent medical school. The city is rich in history, including an occupation by Hitler. Vinnitsa also hosts one of the few remaining Jewish communities in Ukraine — one of the few remaining as the Nazis slaughtered nearly the entire Jewish population (approximately 28,000 people in that region alone) during their occupation. Hitler chose Vinnitsa to be one of his headquarters for the occupation of Ukraine, and situated his bunker, the Werewolf, between the outskirts of the city and a nearby village called Strizhavka. Although much of the Werewolf has been destroyed, enough still stands as a reminder of the evil inflicted by the Nazis on the Ukrainian people.

For as long as history can recount, Ukraine has always been a country with an agricultural bent. With soil as black as a moonless night sky, it is no wonder that some of the best crops in the world come from the soil of Ukraine, and the most fertile regions surround the city of Vinnitsa and the northwestern part of Ukraine.

As I walked the streets of Vinnitsa, my mind could not help but wander to thoughts of Anna's birth parents. How could the poverty be so severe as to lead a family to abandon a child? Not just a family, but thousands of families? Yet, evidence of poverty was just a step behind everything I saw. It was children living in the sewers under the copper manhole covers. It was in the dilapidated buildings behind lovely gardens. It was on the faces of the little elderly ladies selling beautiful flowers on the street corners. I understood that this country of peaceful farmers and thoughtful citizens had survived some of the greatest human rights violations the world has ever seen.

Many of the buildings throughout the city appeared to be built at about the age of World War II, complete with trams that ran on electric wires. Cherry trees lined the streets and flower stands, boasting brilliantly colored flowers, added to the beauty. There were churches, libraries, markets, and parks. However, our link was always strongest to the internet café.

Each morning I eagerly opened the emails that came from family and friends, as their words of encouragement and support were like water to a person lost in the desert.

I read about the antics of Ben and Justin, eating up each bit of news. Ben's predictions about an increase in his consumption of candy had been correct, as evidenced by the five pounds he had gained since we had left. There had been play dates, trips to the movies, the zoo, the museum center, and White Castle for milkshakes. Each day, they opened a small gift from us, and each day they knew that it was one day closer to us coming home. For all my angst, they continued to do quite well without us.

One day, despite our timing with the satellite, it was taking longer than normal to download an email from my mom. After several minutes, it opened to reveal a picture of Ben and Justin with huge smiles on their faces. On a visit to Six Flags, they were hugging Daffy Duck. I had to laugh as I compared my anguish with their revelry.

The picture gave me an idea. Within minutes, the manager of the café had downloaded a picture of Anna and it was traveling back to the US. The next day we received a bulk of emails from those who received the picture and the verdict was unanimous: Anna was beautiful.

One response had especially touched my heart. My father had printed out the picture of Anna and showed it to Ben and Justin. Ben took the picture and stared at it, enamored with his first look at the sister he had been waiting on for years. Then he quietly went over and took down a picture frame that we had given my parents for Christmas. It had space for three pictures, all in a row. The outer two were holding pictures of Ben and Justin, the middle one was empty — waiting for a picture of Anna.

"We need to put Anna's picture in here," Ben told my father.

After cropping the picture on the computer, he printed it out. Ben carefully cut it to the correct size, and together, they put her picture into the frame. And there it was, just as it was always meant to be: Ben, Anna, and Justin.

Doma

There's no place like home!

— Dorothy, *The Wizard of Oz*

Home is a name, a word, it is a strong one; stronger than a magician ever spoke, or spirit ever answered to, in the strongest conjuration. — Charles Dickens

Do not be afraid, for I am with you; I will bring your children from the east and gather you from the west. I will say to the north, "Give them up!" and to the south, "Do not hold them back." Bring my sons from afar and my daughters from the ends of the earth.

— Isaiah 43:5-6 (NIV)

"At that time I will bring you home. I will give you honor and praise among all the peoples of the earth ..." says the Lord. — Zephaniah 3:20 (NIV)

Finally, the day of the guardianship council arrived. We broke our normal routine, and, in lieu of a morning visit to Anna, we went to visit the Regional Inspector. Ira had been working with her for the past several days, making sure that all the paperwork was in order. However, she looked dismayed when she saw us standing in her office.

"The meeting is this evening. Come back in the morning."

The next morning, we rose early and walked back to her office. She was not smiling, but, then again, she never did. She stood up and handed Ira some papers.

"They are approved."

Overjoyed by the news, I was ready to go talk to the judge. I bounded down the dark hallway and almost skipped down the uneven, broken steps. I even knew the way to the courthouse — maybe we could run there. For the past three weeks we had been told, over and over again: The guardianship council must approve you, then you can speak with the judge to set a court date. The guardianship council had spoken, and, as promised, it was time to go to court.

But this was Ukraine, so a few steps had been left out.

"The notary is this way," Ira said, as she broke my optimism.

"Why do we need a notary?" I asked.

"We need to have these documents notarized. Then we need to hire a lawyer to draft a letter for the judge. Then that will have to be notarized. Then we can go to set up an appointment to meet with the judge ... to set the court date."

I resigned myself to the Ukrainian pace of life and followed Ira to the notary's office.

The notary had an office that could only be described as posh. The notary herself looked as though she could've stepped right out of the pages of *Mademoiselle* magazine. Chic clothes, beautiful hair, and lots of makeup. I thought of her in comparison to the little man that had county certified all of our documents back home, and was, once again, amazed by the cultural differences. In the US, one became a notary after filling out some paperwork and swearing an oath. In Ukraine, one became one after five years of college education.

Her office was small, but almost equal in technology to the mayor's. She actually had a computer. Russian disco music played in the background as she diligently worked with our papers for the next hour or so.

We took the papers with us to the courthouse. There we tracked down the office of the public lawyers. It was a dark office with three lawyers working. A woman in the back waved us to her desk. Ira explained our needs and the lawyer took our paperwork. As she began her work she kept talking to Ira, her voice sounding loud and angry. I had no idea what her role was in the adoption process, but I was certain that we did not want her to be angry with us.

"She wants to know why you would adopt such a child as this," Ira said.

Not more interviewing! I thought, *Enough is enough! We've already explained this to so many people. They all take notes — can't they just read each others notes?* I sat there fuming at the thought of going through yet another interview.

Our silence was starting to embarrass Ira. "She is just curious. She is very impressed that you would have a heart that was willing to adopt a child with so many problems."

"Oh!" By this time, I was embarrassed, too. Possibly part of our embarrassment was because neither of us were entirely sure why we would do what we were doing.

"Well, we just wanted to serve God," I started, trying to put it all in words. "We wanted to be more like Jesus is and was when he was on earth. The more we prayed about being like him, the more we understood that God's heart is with children like this little girl. Slowly, he changed our hearts so that what was important to him became important to us. This isn't a burden that we are taking on — it's an honor he's trusting us with."

Far from anything that she had ever thought about before, the lawyer was obviously moved by what God had called us to do. The conversation came to a close, and I began to realize that there was value in some of the delays. It was easy to forget that, as Christians, our purpose of spreading the kingdom of God was as big as the purpose of completing Anna's adoption.

Unfortunately, though, it would take a day for the lawyer to complete the letter to the judge.

We awoke early, ate breakfast, and returned to the lawyer's office.

"The letter is complete," she told us through Ira. "God bless you. I am thankful that God cares enough to send parents for this little girl."

And, with that, we took the letter and, finally, went to talk to the judge's secretary. We moved up a floor and down the hall to wait to see him. There were seven people in line ahead of us. Time moved on and we passed it by watching an older gentleman repair a table that belonged to the courthouse.

"They say, 'Repair the table,' " he told Ira, "but they do not give me the hardware to repair it with. How do you repair a table with no hardware?"

He pulled out a hand tool I had never seen before. It was a tiny chisel and was accompanied by a small mallet. Then he took out an old screw. Meticulously, he rechiseled the cross on the head of the screw. He repeated the process on several more screws. I wondered if someone else's table was going to fall apart when they sat down at it. It was apparent that these screws came from somewhere and it wasn't the supply closet.

Slowly, he worked on each leg of the table. As he began the last one, the secretary called us in. We entered the judge's chamber and he greeted us. Ira handed the judge the paperwork. As he looked through it, he told us that he hoped to set the court date soon. "We try to move adoptions quickly here," he said.

You could've fooled me! I thought, but wisely did not say.

"Come back in the morning, and the secretary will, hopefully have a date for you."

That was it! It was going to take his secretary an entire day to check her book. Of course, for all I knew, she might have to get special stamps and letters of permission to check her book and then get an entirely different set of stamps and permission letters to actually set the date.

We trudged back to the Hotel Savoy, feeling inches closer to the end. I had hoped for real progress today, but consigned myself to the fact that there would probably be some reason that the judge would not have the date for us the next day. An evening of BBC, spades, and the completion my third read through of the *Fellowship of the Ring* followed, and then we went to bed.

Early the next morning we headed back to the courthouse. When we entered the judge's chambers, the secretary smiled and pulled out the schedule book. She and Ira chatted for a minute, and Ira smiled and said, "We go to court tomorrow morning!"

I couldn't believe what I had heard. We had arrived in Ukraine on May 12, and finally, on June 5 we would get to go to court.

I awoke the next morning a nervous bundle of energy. Anything could happen at that court hearing. He could deny the adoption or approve it. If it went well and was approved, the judge could make the decision final. Or we could be told we had to wait another thirty days before he would finalize any decision. Dressed in our best clothes, we headed to the courthouse. As we waited outside the judge's chamber, we were met by the Regional Inspector. Certain that she did not like us, I was worried by her need to be in court.

I had never been to court in my entire life, and I had no idea what to expect. Thanks to some childhood time spent watching *The People's Court* on television, I realized that there was certain protocol as far as standing before the judge and addressing him, but I had no context for anything. I felt completely unprepared. We were relying on Ira's translations and leadership, and I was very aware that Anna's future hung in the balance. I doubt the judge fully understood how much power he held.

We stood as the judge read to the court our petition to adopt. As he called the first witness, the Regional Inspector, we were able to sit down. My hands were shaking in my lap as I watched the hearing proceed. Ira whispered the translations into my ear.

The inspector stood as she addressed the court. She answered several questions and then sat down.

"He asked her several questions about your interest in Anna and how well you followed protocol with the adoption," Ira whispered. "Her answers were all favorable."

The judge then called the orphanage director — she was not there. I worried that her absence would reflect poorly on her opinion of us. The judge made note of it and moved onto the final witnesses: us.

We rose and the judge began to interview us. He quickly moved through the perfunctory paperwork questions and then, addressing me, he asked one question: "Why do you want a child with problems such as this?"

Holding back my tears, I answered, knowing that the answer to this question would play a deciding factor in his decision. "Because we love our children for who they are, not what they look like. God looks at our hearts, not our bodies. The value for life comes from within. This girl is as valuable as any other child, even more so to us, because God has told us that she is ours."

I shook as he took notes. Then he turned to Rob and asked, "You attest to the fact that you can financially provide for her, giving her the same upbringing that you are giving your sons?"

"Yes, there is no doubt we can."

Then he dismissed us to wait in the hallway. The wait felt like an eternity, but in what was only a matter of minutes we were called back in. We stood as he read the court decree.

> *In The Name of Ukraine*
> *June 5 2002*
> *Leninsky District Court of Vinnitsa City*
> *Judge ******* Resolves:*
> *To permit the adoption of Halyna ***** ****** by*
> *Robert and Deborah Amend.*
> *To assign the girl the name and surname:*
> *Anna Halyna Amend*
> *To register as father of the girl Robert L. Amend*
> *To register as mother of the girl Deborah J. Amend*
> *The decision of this court is effective immediately.*

As Ira whispered the translations into my ear, I could no longer hold back the tears. A positive decision — with no more waiting!

"*Diakuyu...*" we said as we shook hands with the judge. Once outside his chamber, the inspector approached us. "God bless you," she said in English. "You have done a good thing." And, then, to my surprise, she hugged me.

It was a truly miraculous day.

The next morning Ira and I dropped Rob off at the train station. He needed to get back to Kyiv to finish some paperwork at the embassy before it closed for the weekend. Then, armed with a cake bought at a local bakery, and Anna's new dress, we took a cab to the orphanage. The children were playing outside when we arrived.

"Halyna," Ira said with a smile, "guess what today is!"

Anna's eyes widened. *"Doma?"*

"We need to say good-bye first."

After giving the cake to the caregivers, I began to walk around the orphanage to take some photographs. All the children were outside, so Anna's section of the orphanage was completely empty. As I looked at the child-sized tables, chairs, and beds, I could imagine each child in their own place. I thought about Anna's bed and seat at the table — which would not be left empty at all. There was already a new child to take her place. I realized how much this place had been home to Anna and how precious the children and the workers were to me. I grieved for the losses that Anna was facing, along with the uncertain future of all the children left behind. Although I had been so eager to leave, it felt very strange to finally go. I was going to miss the Baby House.

But it was time. The long-awaited day had arrived, and this chapter of Anna's life was ending. I was prepared for Anna to be torn between me and the orphanage. Ira had already warned me, "Don't be hurt if she cries about leaving. She is attached to her orphanage, after all they have been her family since she was a baby. Usually the children cry when it is time to leave."

However, Anna never takes the path that most children take! When I came back to the group she jumped into my arms.

Caregivers tried to hug her and hold her, tears in their eyes as they prepared to say good-bye to a child that they loved.

"Nyet!" Anna said as she pushed them away. "My Mama only!" She was terrified that I would leave her behind.

We all walked from the playground to the inside of the orphanage. I set my bag down as I talked to the staff. Out of the corner of my eye, I could see Anna doing a little snooping. She scooted over to my bag and peered into the corner of the department store bag that held her dress, tights, shoes, and undergarments. Trembling with emotion, she ripped open the bag. Then, she pulled out the lavender floral print dress, caressing the silk lining and rubbing her face in the soft fabric.

"Platya!" she whispered — dress.

The quiet was only momentary, though, as the reality of the situation sank in. *"Platya,"* she then cheered, *"Halyna doma!"* Halyna is going home!

With that pronouncement she began to rip the orphanage clothes off her body, layer by layer. I helped her with the tights and shoes and finished the changeover with two barrettes.

"Halyna! You have your dress!" the workers said when they saw her. "You are going home."

"Doma. Halyna doma," she replied, her face glowing and her eyes wide with joy.

As we walked around the orphanage, Anna was given many tearful hugs and kisses good-bye. She, however, gripped my shoulder, unwilling to let go lest I forget to take her with me.

"Paka!" she yelled as we walked out the door. Bye-bye! "I am now going home ... to *America* ... with *my Mama* ... riding in *my stroller.* I am not sure where my Papa is, but I do have one somewhere! Bye-bye!"

For the last time, I walked down the street that led to the orphanage. The cherry trees were in full season and the street was littered with cherries that had fallen on their own. A chicken ran past, a dog barked, and I heard a couple arguing in Russian behind one of the fences that lined the street. The sun shone and there was a gentle breeze. It was like many spring days in Ukraine, but this one was different.

This time, I was *finally* bringing Anna home.

That afternoon Ira, Anna, and I boarded the train to leave Vinnitsa. Anna, having never seen anything beyond her orphanage walls, was overwhelmed by what she saw. As we entered the train, a conductor kindly took one side of her stroller in order to help me carry it up the steps onto the train. "Hey ... back off! It's my stroller," she told him. Thankfully, I had no idea what she said, so Ira was embarrassed for me.

We were the first people on the train, and as we settled into our seats, Anna was very content to look out the window and climb on my lap. That is, until other passengers started entering and taking their seats.

"What are you doing here?" she yelled. "This is my train. You need to leave it since you did not ask me. This is *my* train. *My* Mama gave it to me. You need to leave."

Ira explained to her the rightful ownership of the train. She was truly disappointed but willing to be diplomatic about it.

"All right," she said in her usual loud voice. "You can all stay on the train, but just remember who it really belongs to."

The train whizzed along the tracks, and, once again, I tried to memorize the landscape. I wanted to be able to tell Anna about every plant, every tree, every farm — everything I could about her homeland. Anna was amazed at the sights, but like any good three-year-old, she soon tired of being in one place and looking out the window. Restless, she sat on my lap and talked to Ira.

"Do you believe in the Bye-Bye Monster?" she asked Ira, referring to the old Russian folk tales about *Baba Yaga* — a witch who lives in a hut that stands on owl's feet and delights in eating small children.

"No," Ira replied.

"Does my Mama believe in the Bye-Bye Monster?"

"No."

"Does my Papa believe in the Bye-Bye Monster?"

"No."

"Well, *I* believe in the Bye-Bye Monster."

135

Ira and I laughed at the strength of her pronouncement, unaware of how incredibly strong that belief was.

We arrived in Kyiv and met Rob at the apartment. Anna was overjoyed at seeing her Papa again, and we settled in for the night. After dinner, we gave her her first bath. The hot water in our entire complex was turned off for yearly servicing (and would remain so for the rest of the time that I was there). This was nice, in that it meant that we did not have to listen to the hot water gush in the kitchen sink anymore, but it was terrible when it came time to bathe and shower.

For about forty minutes, I heated water in pots on the stove. Then I carefully carried the pots across the apartment to the bathtub and added it to the freezing cold water. Anna watched in amazement as I filled the tub.

"Vanna. Bath."

"Vanna," she replied.

Her caregivers told us that she was given a bath approximately once a year. Daily cleaning was done with a hose that attached to the sink in the bathroom. They would squirt her off with cold water, cleaning the parts that were dirty from her day. Although she had enjoyed the last bath that she had, it had been over a year ago, and I wasn't certain how she would react.

Gently I lifted her into the tub. She looked up at me in surprise. "Water!"

"Yes! A bath is full of water ... *vanna* ... *voda....*"

She scooped the water up in a cup and watched it flow back in with the rest. She splashed. She scooted and laid in it. Then she created her own little bath time song, sung to the tune of a song we heard the children sing at the orphanage. *"Vanna, vanna, va-nna .... Vanna, vanna, va-nna...."* She played until bedtime.

We laid her down on a bed that was in the same room we slept in. Her eyes were huge, with big tears. I sat next to her and laid my hand on her chest. Her heart was racing. She was sweating profusely (something I later learned was a physical sign that her body was in shock over the changes she was experiencing). She looked terrified.

Unable to leave her side, Rob sat with her until she fell asleep.

Several days later, Anna and I boarded an airplane bound for Warsaw, Poland. Rob, needing to return to the USA in order to keep his job, had left Kyiv several days earlier. I had completed all Ukrainian aspects of the adoption and was due to finish her immigration paperwork at the US Embassy in Warsaw. As the plane took off and left the Borispol airport, Anna and I looked out the window. Enthralled with the airplane, and naive about all she was leaving, Anna was only fascinated with the landscape. I, however, felt my heart rip in two as we flew further and further away from my daughter's birth country and heritage.

The line went down the street and around the corner. I thought that when I said good-bye to Ukraine, I had said good-bye to lines, but I was certainly wrong. We had been dropped off by cab at the entrance to the US embassy in Warsaw. However, as I followed the line to its end, I realized that it was going to be hours before we would even enter the embassy. If we did not get to the visa interview today, then we would be stuck in Warsaw over the weekend and our flights would have to be rescheduled (for what would be the third time!).

I surveyed the line and looked for other Americans, but couldn't find any.

"Are you waiting for a visa interview?" I asked the young lady in front of me.

"Yes," she replied, with a very heavy accent. "Immigrant visa interview."

I sighed as I pondered this problem. I could not possibly wait in this line. There were over 100 people in front of me, from all parts of Eastern Europe, all hoping to be granted an immigrant visa. Anna was simply another immigrant waiting and hoping.

But, I thought, *she has something that they don't.*

On a whim, I left my place in line, rounded the corner and walked down the street to the security booth that marked the entrance of the embassy. I walked up to the booth and knocked on the window. One of the security guards looked at me and scowled. I held up my US passport, and his scowl turned to a smile, and he waved us in the door. Within minutes we were filling out the forms for Anna's visa interview. Later that day, we returned, flashed the passport again, and picked up the last of the paperwork.

The adoption was completed. Now we just had to get home.

We rose early the next morning and arrived at the airport at 4:30 a.m. There we flew from Warsaw to Amsterdam, waited eight hours for our next flight (the transatlantic flight). By the time we were scheduled to board, both Anna and I were exhausted beyond anything I had ever experienced.

The airline asked people with small children to board first. It was then that I made a grave mistake. I complied. Those with small children do not need to board a plane an hour before take off — it only serves to extend the time that the child is stuck on the plane. Still naive, though, I did what they said. It soon went south.

Not long after getting settled, we were told that the auxiliary power unit that ran the air conditioning while the plane was on the ground was broken. The plane began to heat up, and we continued to wait as people boarded the plane. And, as we heated up, so did poor little, overstimulated Anna. I had suspicions that she had a temper in her, and those suspicions were about to be confirmed. There had been too many changes, too little sleep, far too many airplanes, and she had had enough.

"*NYYYYYEEEETTTT!*" she yelled, at the top of her lungs.

All of a sudden, she decided that she did not, under any circumstances, want to be on anymore airplanes. I tried every trick in the book to calm her down. But it was to no avail. She was hot, tired, overstimulated, and confused. She wanted one thing, and it was the one thing that I could not give her: She wanted off the plane.

I, too, was hot, tired, overstimulated, and simply defeated. Finally, I set her in the seat next to me and just let her cry. I had been a mommy long enough to know that no child could cry forever — although it was obvious that my child was going to try her best!

138

A woman sitting in front of us heightened my stress by peri-odically turning around and glaring at me. I knew that she was angry at Anna's loudness, but there was nothing I could do to stop her. I simply opened a magazine and started to flip through it. The woman continued to glare at me.

I was at a loss as to what to do. I couldn't get off the plane. I couldn't even really communicate anything to Anna. She was very mad at me and did not want my comfort. In fact, when I held her it was worse. She needed to fall into a deep sleep. I sat next to her and let her cry. This went on for several minutes until, finally, the woman got up and asked a flight attendant if she could switch seats. Gathering up her belongings, she gave me a final glare and parting words,

"You, ma'am, are the most selfish person in the world. People should not subject other people to their crying, screaming children just so they can take vacations around the world."

With that she stormed off. My hands tied, and my mind com-pletely fried, I sat there and did the only thing that I could do. I cried.

The plane took off, and within twenty minutes, Anna was sound asleep. She slept for the entire flight. I relaxed as much as I could, and dozed off and on for the remainder of the flight. My sleep, however, was somewhat disturbed by a screaming infant. I did fair better than my former seatmate, though, as, when she switched her seat she did not notice the sleeping infant directly in front of her.

Our plane landed in Detroit and, as the wheels of the plane hit the ground, my eyes filled with tears again. This time, though, it was because the moment those wheels hit the pavement, Anna be-came a US citizen.

We exited the plane, went through customs and a brief inter-view with INS, and then off to our connector flight. Anna was so tired she slept through the entire flight. Peace filled my entire be-ing as each minute brought me closer to home. Now back in the US, I felt that I was done. I could, once again, relax.

When the plane landed at Cincinnati, I woke Anna up. "Do you want to see Papa? Ben? Justin? They will all be there to meet you!"

We gathered our belongings and I put Anna in the stroller. As we walked down the concourse, I became more and more excited. It was June 16. I left home on May 12. I could not wait to hold my sons again. We exited the tarmac and I was nearly running. We went past security and then I saw them.

They were at the end of the hall and my parents and Rob were with them. Ben was holding a balloon that said, "I love you," and Justin was holding a balloon with a picture of an American flag. I ran to meet them, dropped to my knees, and as I hugged them I cried without stopping. I couldn't believe it was over.

The boys were glad to see me, but they really wanted to meet their new sister. I picked her up and began the introductions. "Ben and Justin, this is your sister, Anna."

They each gave her a balloon, which we tied to her stroller, and then gave her a quick hug.

"Anna, this is your Grandma and Grandpa. Babushka and Dedushka." Anna willingly went to my mom.

"Grandma," my mom told her, pointing to herself.

Anna looked at her and said, "Gamma."

Through all this, though, Anna wanted her Papa. "Papa" she said, over and over again, as she touched his face.

We put her back in the stroller and Ben pushed her to the car. Then, Anna, who only days before had no family to call her own, rode home with her mom, dad, brothers, and grandparents.

There was no question that it had all been worth it.

Baba Yaga And Pining For The Good Ol' Days

The pain passes but the beauty remains.
— Pierre Auguste Renoir

In order to emerge from a state of loss and grief, and begin a new life, people need not so much a therapist as friends who are prepared to walk with them.
— Attributed to Jean Vanier

There is a time for everything, and a season for every activity under heaven: a time to be born and a time to die, a time to plant and a time to uproot, a time to kill and a time to heal, a time to tear down and a time to build, a time to weep and a time to laugh, a time to mourn and a time to dance.
— Ecclesiastes 3:1-4 (NIV)

Ben uttered his first sentence when he was eighteen months old. We were at the grocery store, waiting at the checkout, and he was watching in fascination an older boy who was spinning around in circles as he waited for his mother. Ben pointed his little pudgy finger at the boy and said his first complete sentence: "The boy spins round and round!"

Justin spoke his first sentence at 22 months of age. He walked into our kitchen and saw his brother eating a piece of cheese. Outraged that his brother had something to eat and he didn't, he was motivated to speak his first complete sentence: "I want cheese, too!"

Anna had been home for four weeks when she spoke her first complete English sentence. We had just sat down for dinner. All of our plates had been filled, and drinks served. "Potty?" she asked, right after we had finished our prayer.

"Sure," I replied, and she started to climb out of her booster seat. Stopping halfway down, she balanced rather precariously on her stomach so she could shake her index finger at her brothers. It was then she said her first sentence, and she said it loud and clear: "Ben and Justin, don't eat my food or drink my kool-aid."

English came very quickly for her, and within a month she was saying sentences in half English and half Russian.

"*Ya nee* (I no) pee in pants ..." she would say if she was making a mad dash to the bathroom.

"*Ya nee* time out ..." if she got in trouble.

We often found ourselves answering questions in her peculiar mix of Russian and English.

"Justin, would you like something to drink?"

"*Da*, but *nyet molokoh!*" (Yes, but no milk.)

Or, when explaining the sequence of events, we always used Anna's own phrase "*e* and then," "*e*" being the Russian word for "and."

"First we will go to church, *e and then* we will get lunch."

It was enough to make any good Ukrainian shake their head in shame and say, *"Ai ai ai."* Thankfully, our slaughter of the Russian language did not last very long. By the time she had been home for two months, only two Russian words were left in her vocabulary: *molokoh* (milk) and *doma* (home). It was apparent from the beginning that most of her thoughts centered on food. It was a logical focus, if you consider how greatly her circumstances had changed.

While still in Ukraine, Anna and I had gone out to lunch with a group of people from the church. Most were American, but one man who was Ukrainian, came with us. He talked with Anna through most of the meal and was able to ask her questions for me.

"Ask her what she ate at the orphanage," I said.

He and Anna spoke for a couple minutes.

"Porridge," he replied.

"What else?" I asked, and so he asked her.

"She said, 'Porridge, just only porridge.' "

Although she probably did eat some other foods as well, the blood work that we had done on her when she arrived home certainly backed up what she said. She was anemic, had mild rickets, and several vitamin deficiencies. Further testing showed us that it was all related to diet. Her behavior toward food provided further evidence, as well.

Each day was started with the same routine. Anna and the boys would wake up and get dressed. I would brush her hair, help her with her chores, and we would all head down to the kitchen. The boys would take their seat at the table and wait for breakfast, but Anna always had an additional chore that she had assigned herself.

She would walk over to the refrigerator and, using all her strength, pry open the door. Then, eyeing everything inside, she would make her daily pronouncement: "We still have food." Then, she would take her seat with her brothers, careful not to sit too close, in case they would try to take her food. In their defense, they never even tried once.

Confused as to why we would eat anything except ice cream and bananas (since they were so good, why even bother with the other stuff?), food was her most talked about subject, with, maybe the exception of milk. She loved her *molokoh* and drank nearly an entire gallon a day. She loved us all, and she and her brothers got along very well. In fact, they were best of friends, except at mealtimes, when Anna viewed them, her Papa, and me all as her adversaries.

"Justin, would you like some more potatoes?" I asked.

"Sure," he replied.

"Well," Anna interrupted, "don't take all of it."

143

"Anna, there is plenty left."

"I know. But don't take all of it."

"I would like some more salad, could someone please pass it?"

"You can have more," Anna answered, "but don't take all of it."

This continued for months, until, one night Rob had had enough. As he was serving himself some food, Anna started in on her usual mini-lecture: "Now Daddy, don't take all of it."

He froze, serving bowl in one hand, spoon in the other. Then, looking at Anna the entire time, he dumped the remaining food onto his plate. She looked truly shocked. "I can take all of it and that's okay. There will always be more."

Sometimes we would worry that she would choke. She was not used to so many different foods, and it seemed as though she was not even sure how to chew some things. If there were any other children around, she would cram food into her mouth until her cheeks would puff out, afraid that someone would snatch up what was not in her mouth. She had an anxiety about food that only time and a steady supply could heal. And, there were times when it produced some very hilarious scenes.

The first time I took her grocery shopping with me, she was so overwhelmed by all the food that she was, surprisingly enough, speechless. She sat in the cart, with a completely dumbfounded look on her face, her eyes as wide as saucers. This speechless expression continued until we reached the dairy section, where she saw, sitting on shelves on the back wall, more jugs of milk than she could count.

"Molokoh! Molokoh! Odeen, Dvah, Trie, cheterie, pyat...." Milk! Milk! One, two, three, four, five....

Only able to count to five, she counted again and again, nearly falling out of the cart with excitement. Her joy over milk was almost equal to her love of American toilet paper — which she would always insist on hugging as she sat in the cart.

Another time, just about a month after she came home, my parents came into town for visit. As the boys love to go to buffet-style restaurants, they offered to take us out for lunch. I carried her

144

up to the buffet, unaware of the impact that three large buffet tables would have on her. When her gaze hit the tables, she could not contain her joy. She started hugging me and telling me over and over, "Thank you, Mama! I love you! Thank you, Mama! I love you!"

For someone to go from, "Porridge, just only porridge," to a feast of this kind was nothing short of miraculous.

It took her almost a year to finally understand how to handle food. She grew to understand that she needed to eat a variety of things and it began to feel normal to have a full stomach. One day, though, it all came into focus when she, for the first time, tried a food that she didn't like. It was a green olive, and as she chewed it, the look on her face told us she needed to spit it out as quickly as possible. However, despite the fact that it was making her sick, she continued to chew the olive. Finally, Rob told her to spit it out.

Slowly and uneasily she walked over to the garbage can. She looked at us one last time and spit it out. Her eyes were large, and she looked very guilty.

"Sweetheart," Rob told her, "it's okay to spit out a food that you don't like. Everybody has food that they don't like. You don't have to keep it in your mouth!"

"If you don't like a food, you don't have to eat it." She repeated, and I was thankful that, now, that was a reality in her life.

Anna also went through shock. She would sweat so profusely that she would soak through several shirts in one day. Some days, the sweat was so thick I had to bathe her twice to keep her clean. She regressed in her potty training and would wake up from her naps screaming and sobbing.

Even more overwhelming than that was when she threw royal temper tantrums in response to something she didn't like. Apparently, she had been led to believe that America was the land flowing with milk and honey — a land where a little girl would get anything her heart desired. The reality of the misconception hit her the first day she arrived home.

"Mommm!" Ben yelled to me from the other room. "Anna pinched me!"

I rushed into our family room and found a tragic scene. Little Anna stood over her big brother, holding his toy giraffes, while Ben held his right arm, crying. Thinking that he must be overreacting, I bent down to examine his arm. Sure, enough, there were two deep nail-sized indentations, red and swollen, where his sister had pinched him.

"Anna Halyna," I said, with scorn in my voice, "You don't pinch!"

Anna looked at me with great innocence, her eyes implying that it was all a misunderstanding.

"And," I continued, "you have to give Ben his giraffes back."

The innocence turned to shock. Obviously, she wanted those giraffes as that was why she pinched him in the first place. Looking straight in her eyes, I took the giraffes and gave them back to Ben.

"*Dolia*. Share."

Anna looked at me, completely offended at what I had said. Then she let me know exactly what she was thinking, even though she did not have the English to express it. She screamed — for the next three hours. In fact, she fell asleep on the floor right in the spot where she started her tantrum. When she awoke, she was back to being my little angel.

These tantrums were frequent. They were so frequent, in fact, that many people would comment to us that Anna had the "cutest little husky Russian voice." Rob and I would just smile at each other when that happened. "Ya ... it's just a husky Russian voice."

Then there was the Bye-Bye Monster. I had read enough to know that we were not the first adoptive parents that had to slay *Baba Yaga*. Over the years, I had heard stories about her. Sometimes adopted children would worry that their new mommies were *Baba Yaga* in disguise, as, in their imaginations, the red fingernail polish that they had never seen before became the blood of previously eaten children. Some orphanages, in a desperate attempt to keep little ones in bed at night tell the children that *Baba Yaga* is there looking for a boy or girl to eat. However, if you lay still and close your eyes, then she is not able to see you.

We never found out exactly what Anna was told about *Baba Yaga*, but, whatever it was, the fable was very real to her, and, while all the words may have become lost in her new language, the fear followed her.

"I can't go to sleep."

"Why?"

"There is that bad guy outside my window that wants to eat me!"

"But there are no bad guys that want to eat people," I replied, thinking that she would probably avoid any cannibalistic serial killers, so, technically, this was not a lie.

"Well, I know there is. He is an ugly, bad guy that looks like a witch. He wants to eat me."

"Well, even if there was, God has angels that protect you, and he sent us Sammy to protect you, too."

Sammy, our border collie, was Anna's best friend, and she was certain that Sammy would gladly give her life to battle any bad guy in order to protect her. We never let her know that, in the case of an intruder, Sammy was far more likely to hide behind her than to protect her.

Each night for a year, we would have this conversation, which would follow with a prayer for protection. And, still, even with that, she would lay down with fear in her eyes.

Over time, though, the bad guy began to change. Maybe it was Anna's prayers.

> *Dear Lord Jesus,*
> *I pray for the bad guy who wants to eat me. I pray*
> *that he will meet you and you will change his heart.*
> *Then he will be a good guy who doesn't want to eat*
> *children. Amen.*

Soon, he no longer ate people, he just stole their toys. Then, he just broke their favorite things. Eventually, he either found Jesus, or he found another family to torment, because Anna forgot him. And, we were very glad.

I had expected her to begin grieving the day we left the orphanage. I knew that she was attached to her caregivers and friends, and I was thankful that she was. That attachment was a key component to surviving the changes ahead, for if she attached there, she could transfer that attachment to us. That day, though, she never saw what she was losing. At the age of three, she could only see what she was gaining, and she left the orphanage not completely understanding that it was good-bye for good. It was a concept that, over time, she began to comprehend.

When a parent has only had boys and adopts a girl, the most popular gift to give is a baby doll. Anna came home to a room full of perfect little baby dolls and all the accoutrements that go with them. I wondered how she would play house with so many babies. But, of course, she did not know how to play house, so she played what she knew: orphanage.

"This one," she pointed to the first baby, "Luba. This one Tonya. This Natasha. Andrushka, Edik ..." and so it continued until she had named all the children in her group at the orphanage.

Each one she would, feed, rock, swaddle, and serenade with little Ukrainian folk songs. She was very diligent in her care for her friends, and I loved to watch her.

"You know," I told her, "you're my baby."

"Yes," she would reply as she hugged me. "Mama."

Then she would go back to caring for her babies. At the time, I thought that she must just be a very maternal little girl. But now that I know her (she is a girl who currently only has maternal feelings for puppies and ponies), I realize that she wasn't caring for her children, she was providing for her friends.

"When can you adopt Luba and Tonya?" she asked me one day.

"We cannot adopt them ..." I started to explain, unsure of how to express the details of adoption laws to a three-year-old.

Or when out among friends and family, many people would often pose the same question.

"Do you think you'll adopt more?"

"Yes, of course," Anna would pipe up, "we will adopt Luba and Tonya!"

She would draw pictures of her friends and save portions of her food for them. Daily, she tried to convince us to go back and adopt them. We did our best to explain the situation to her, but it was never good enough.

One day, all three kids were sitting at the table drawing. Anna drew a circle. She pointed at it.

"Sun."

Then she drew a line.

"Slide."

Then she drew a circle with some lines.

"Luba. Bye-bye, Luba."

Then another of the same.

"Tonya. Bye-bye, Tonya."

Then another.

"Natasha. Bye-bye, Natasha."

She did this again and again until she had said good-bye to all her friends. I hugged her and told her that she was such a good friend. I had a suspicion that she had begun to understand the big picture ... at least as much as a three-year-old could.

Several weeks later, at bedtime, the issue came up again.

"When do I go back to Ukraine to see Luba? Tomorrow?"

"Well, sweetie." I said, "Ukraine is very far away. I do not know when we can go back. It costs so much money to go there and it is so far away."

She thought for a few minutes and said, "Well, we could drive our van."

"No, we can't. There is a big ocean between us and Ukraine. You cannot drive a van on the ocean."

She lay down and said her prayers. I hoped that I had answered her questions enough. However, several days later, it came up again.

"Grandma and Grandpa live far away and we drive the van there. So, we can drive the van to Ukraine. You lie to me."

"There is no ocean between Grandma and us. There is an ocean between us and Ukraine. We cannot go back there now, but we can pray for your friends."

So, we prayed and she went to sleep. I realized that the issue encompassed everything from trust to basic geography, and somehow I knew that it was not going to be easily solved. I soon found out that I was right.

Since arriving home, part of our nightly bedtime ritual had been us discussing how God had brought her to our family. She would listen to the story with a smile on her face. However, one night, the story was no longer acceptable.

"Don't," she told me. "Don't say God brought me here."

"Why?" I asked.

"I don't like it. God didn't bring me here. He didn't."

I was shocked at her change of heart, but willing to let it go.

Several days later, she scooted up next to me while I was doing the dishes. She had a toy phone with her, pretended to make a phone call, and in her loudest talking voice held a pretend conversation. "Hi, Luba! It is me, Anna ... yes, yes, I miss you, too ... I would like to visit but I can't ... I have a mean, mean, mean, mean mommy and she won't let me visit you."

I set my dishes down and quickly left the room. Sitting down on our couch, I put my head in my hands and cried. I knew that she would say things like that, and I thought that I had prepared myself. But then, when she said it, it *really* hurt. The pain came not only because of all that we had done to bring her home, but because I understood the depth of her loss. It was not the first time that I was hit with grief over her pain, and, I knew that it would not be the last. It was the job that I signed on for.

I pulled myself together and walked back into the kitchen. I kissed her on the head, and said, "I know you are angry with me, but I still love you. I am very sorry you miss Luba and your friends."

Then, came the days of pining for the "good life" in Ukraine.

"Anna, it's time to turn off the TV."

"Hmmp ... In Ukraine, Mama Luba let me watch PBS kids all day long."

Or, when it was time for a nap: "In Ukraine, we didn't nap. We just watched *Lion King* while Mama Luba rested."

In fact, I was informed that they always ate hot dogs and ice cream and were never told to eat their vegetables. They never had to brush their teeth, could eat as much candy as they wanted to, and did not have to use both sides of their paper when drawing pictures. Each time, I would gently correct her, making sure that she didn't build up an imaginary fantasy world in Ukraine.

"Well, you never watched *Lion King* at the orphanage because they did not have it there. They did love to act out folk tales with you, though. Mama Luba told me you were a great actress!"

Or ... "Well, really you ate *kasha* at every meal. You did not get much variety, but the Mamas there loved you and made sure you did not go without food. Sometimes they even brought you food from their own homes!"

Those were the days that tested my patience. I had prepared myself for being compared to her birthmother, but I had never thought that I would lose when being compared to an orphanage. Finally, all of that came to a head though. One morning, at breakfast, I heard quiet crying. It was Anna.

"What's wrong, sweetie?" Rob asked her.

"I will never see Luba and Tonya ever again." Then came the weeping and the sobbing.

I pulled her onto my lap and held her. She sobbed for a long while. There was nothing that we could say. We could not erase the loss that was there. She had gained so much, but, too, she had lost so much. Now, finally, the reality of that set in. After a long time, she calmed down and wiped her eyes.

She looked at me, and said, "I will never see Luba and Tonya again, but I can pray for them that God will take care of them like he takes care of me."

And with that, she reorganized her life. Our time in Ukraine, though so difficult, helped us to understand what she had lost. She hadn't just lost her language and culture, she had lost her first family.

Flight Of The Bumblebee

It must be hard to be a person who has a disability.
Glad I don't. — Anna Amend, seven years old

Aerodynamically the bumblebee shouldn't be able to
fly, but the bumblebee doesn't know that so it goes on
flying anyway.
— Mary Kay Ash, American business woman

To keep me from becoming conceited because of these
surpassingly great revelations, there was given me a
thorn in my flesh ... Three times I pleaded with the Lord
to take it away from me. But he said to me, "My grace
is sufficient for you, for my power is made perfect in
weakness." Therefore I will boast all the more gladly
about my weaknesses, so that Christ's power may rest
on me ... For when I am weak, then I am strong.
— 2 Corinthians 12:7-10 (NIV)

The orphanage doctor stood before me, holding up a very small
x-ray of Anna's legs. The blurred image conveyed little information,

but the doctor pointed to sections of it, indicating the obvious problems with Anna's legs.

"Her right hip socket is missing. The legs are correctable." A gold tooth flashed at me as she smiled. "Simply have a doctor build her a right hip socket and lengthen the right leg. Then they will be fine."

As far as she was concerned, the case was closed. We simply needed to lengthen a leg and build a hip socket, and Anna would have no further issues with her legs. Both of Anna's legs appeared small, and her feet turned out rather than pointing forward. Even with the doctor's positive outlook, I couldn't believe that it would be that simple. I knew there must be missing information.

That afternoon, Rob and I spent several hours in the internet café searching the web for answers about Anna's disabilities. Before long we became convinced that the worst case scenario was that she would need a prosthetic leg. Far from home, in Ukraine, simply struggling to get her home, the concept of prosthetic legs didn't seem so overwhelming. And, it was only a possibility, not a certainty, that a doctor couldn't surgically correct them.

Surely, I thought, *God has plans for this child*, but once home in the United States, our perspective changed.

After our first visit with an American orthopedist, we learned the entire truth.

"The condition's called PFFD (Proximal Focal Femural Deficiency)," he said as he studied the x-rays. "It's absolutely amazing that she can compensate like she does. I, honestly, can't understand how her ankles can even bear her weight."

We sat in shock as he proceeded to explain to us everything that was wrong with our daughter's legs.

"First of all, she has no hip socket on her right side." He pointed to the x-ray, and it was very obvious that he wasn't lying. "Not only no hip socket, but, really no hip. Her muscles are creating a false hip socket."

I sat there, confounded that I hadn't noticed it in Ukraine. She wasn't just missing the socket; there was absolutely no bone where her right hip was supposed to be.

"There are bones missing in her knees, ankles, and feet. Four toes ... pretty significant."

I thought back to how Rob and I joked about her missing toes. Apparently that was a bit more important than we thought.

"Missing toes," he continued, "are always a symptom of something. In this case, her fibulas are missing."

I stared at the x-ray in complete amazement. Although this x-ray was much clearer than the ones we saw in Ukraine, I couldn't believe that I missed this the first time I saw those x-rays of her legs.

Everyone has two shin bones, not one, I thought, *how many model skeletons have I put together with the boys, and yet I never noticed that she only had one shin bone when I saw her x-rays?*

It was too much information at one time, and I was having a terrible time processing it all. And, to make matters worse, he wasn't finished.

"Of course, you realize that all the problems are the same on the left side as well. Just not as severe." He pointed to the x-ray. "She does have a hip over there, however, it's twisted and missing several parts. The fibula is missing as well. The thigh is shortened on this side, but not so much as the right."

Both legs! I thought to myself. *Both legs are affected?*

In reality, I had always known. The first moment I meet Anna, I knew that her legs were much more severe than the orphanage staff was presenting them to be. I just wasn't able to deal with the entire reality of her situation. I had been coasting along, just trying to get my little girl home. Now I could no longer avoid the truth; we were not going to simply build a hip socket, lengthen a leg, and move on with our lives. This was going to be a lasting problem. The problem didn't center on her lack of a hip. The problem was that, as her legs grew, the length discrepancy would grow larger, and, eventually, she would not be able to walk.

In addition to that, as her body grew larger and heavier, it would place more stress on her already weak knees and ankles. In all likelihood, they would grow unable to support the weight of her body, resulting in painful stress fractures. In fact, even the weight of her tiny three-year-old frame was an issue.

"She is truly amazing. She defies physics. Those ankles really shouldn't be able to bear weight at all. Her knees are weak, and the range of motion ... It's just not a range of motion that can produce walking."

He was talking, but I was no longer listening. I couldn't think past what he had just said was missing. I tried to focus my thoughts as he continued.

"Most children with this amount of bone missing never walk — despite years of therapy and intervention. They just simply can't do it. She's really an amazing little girl!"

Over the course of the next few months, we continued to take her to various doctors, and received the same opinions from them all: Anna is a miracle. But what I heard was slightly different. Unable to deal with the losses, I couldn't hold onto what was miraculous. The thought that raced through my mind was: *There's no explanation as to why she can walk, and no promise that she will continue to do so.*

There was so much for us to process at one time. There were two possible surgical options presented to us: amputation followed by fitting with prosthesis, or the arduous process of limb lengthening. Then, any of those possibilities could be turned into multiple options when applied to either just her little leg or both legs. Through it all, my mind could focus on only one thing. The missing thigh bone created a height discrepancy. Anna's body was out of proportion to her legs. My daughter had a form of dwarfism.

I've found it amazing that in light of everything we were facing, all I could think about was Anna's height. Despite the fact that she had the same body she had always had since the day that we met her, I just couldn't get past the fact that my daughter was going to be very short. I thought about the teenage years and all the years leading up to it. I thought about the *Wizard of Oz*, *Austin Powers*, and any number of movies and television shows with little people.

I had plans for her future, and those plans didn't involve an exceptionally short stature. So, as my mind avoided the real issues, I focused on her loss of height, and sought ways to correct that.

The first doctor that mentioned limb lengthening declared her one of the best candidates that he had ever seen. So, we decided to look into that possibility. And, I, in an effort to deal with her "height issues" determined to make it work, despite the fact that it sounded like torture.

While it's true that doctors have grown teeth and bones in a laboratory, no doctor has yet to find a painless and safe way for generating new bones in humans. The existing method, developed by a Russian doctor, involves attaching a metal fixator, called an *Ilazarov* (named after its inventor) to the bone to be lengthened. The process involves inserting metal pins into the existing bone. The pins then protrude through the skin and attach to the metal fixator. The fixator is tightened with a wrench at set times throughout the day. The painless pressure from the tightening puts incremental pressure on the bone causing it to crack and then fill in with new bone. Thus, it stimulates growth of new bone at a rate of about one centimeter per month.

To grow Anna's right leg to the same length as the left would take one year. To grow them to the height that was proportional to her body would take nearly two years — two years of lying down, taking sponge baths, and an incredibly high risk of infection. Then, there was always looming ahead of us the possibility that, after all that, her ankles would not support the weight of her body, and we would end up amputating her feet and fitting with her with prosthetic legs.

Even though I desired to grow Anna to the "right height," we soon realized that we couldn't put her through limb lengthening. As things stood, she could walk. To lengthen her legs would rob her of that for a few years and put her through things that she would never even begin to understand. At the same time, amputation was final, and we couldn't face the possibility of removing her foot without her understanding why.

While we were trying to decide what to do, she was given a metal shoe lift by Shriner's Hospital. The lift, unique in design, was attached to the bottom of her shoe and made her legs the same length when she walked. The improvement in her walking was evident from the first few minutes she wore it. We knew it bought us time to decide.

Still, while we were pondering our next step, I was dealing with my unfounded grief over her height. I just couldn't get past the fact that she was going to be exceptionally little. I prayed for a solution. I prayed for healing. I waited for an answer. And, one day, it finally came. But it didn't come in Anna, it came in me.

"I worry that she won't get married. I had plans for this girl! She has plans!" I told Rob.

"Who said she won't ever get married?" he replied. "I'm sure that there are many little people who are married."

"Who would she marry?" I asked.

"With her personality, someone who's really brave, I think."

"What if she marries someone really tall?" I countered.

"What? So what? That would make things pretty interesting." He was just not very serious about this issue.

"Well," I said, "what if she marries someone else who's really little?"

"Then, I guess we will have lots of little people in our family," he pointed out, with a grin. The thought of having a family of little people was not something either of us had considered.

"It's different, but we both think different is good."

I pondered what he said and pondered Anna living a happy life with a very little man. The thought brought a smile to my face. It was certainly not how I had pictured Christmas dinner in our golden years.

"Plus," Rob added, "being little is just part of being her. She is big in personality and small in stature. She'll make a good corporate lawyer. Those companies will never know what hit 'em."

And then a thought hit me. I was worried about an Anna that I didn't know, not the Anna that I now knew. God had provided for her through so much already, would he just stop when she was thirteen? Would her life not be as fulfilling at four feet tall as it would have been at 5'5"?

I was ashamed to admit it, but the person that needed healed was not Anna. It was me. God was working miracles through my little girl, and all I could do was grieve a loss of height. That night, God not only healed me, but he forgave me for my own shortsightedness and shallowness. He knew what I acknowledged that night.

Anna was perfect the way that she was.

Over the next year, we had several visits to the orthopedist. Each time, a bit more intervention was added until she had a total of three orthotic devices: two braces and a large shoe lift. She walked with great ease; yet I worried about her future.

"At some point, the length discrepancy will be too big to be accommodated with the lift," a doctor told us. "As she grows, her legs will not grow in proportion to each other. She's missing most of the growth element in her right leg."

We processed what the doctor was saying, trying to understand what this would mean. It had taken a year, but I had finally come to acknowledge what would be the best course of action for her right leg. Although it felt as though it ripped my heart in two, I had to come to grips with the fact that, at some point, Anna was going to have to have her right foot amputated.

Way back in Ukraine, when I first entertained the possibility of amputation, I thought that I was okay with it. Now that it was becoming a reality, I was finding that pill much harder to swallow.

The logic was there. Amputate the front part of her foot, and fuse her ankle and knee joints (which are missing so much that they do not function well anyway) and turn her right leg into a stump. Her right foot was currently even with her knee, but would eventually be slightly higher than it. That would allow for a prosthetic leg with a working knee — the best type to have.

But, just because the logic is there doesn't mean that the emotion follows it.

How can I cut off her foot? I raged at God. *Why can't you just heal her?*

Of all the possibilities that I had considered, I had never considered that we would truly face having to amputate part of our daughter's body. There was no peace in my mind, and I grieved for yet another loss that Anna would face.

"Surgery's likely in her future," the doctor said as he watched her, "but when, I can't say. And, there's no reason why she can

walk now, so there's no way to say how long she will be able to ...
maybe a year ... maybe the rest of her life."

"But," I faltered for words, "I just worry about her mobility ..."

I was interrupted though, by Anna. "Watch this, doctor, watch
me jump."

She proceeded to jump from one end of the room to the other,
and then climbed right up onto the examining table.

"I ... mmm ... don't think that mobility is much of an issue for
her."

It was then that I realized that he was right. Again, I was worrying about Anna in the future, not Anna now. Anna right now
could walk, run, jump, climb, and dance. God who had provided
her with the grace and spirit she needed to survive three years in an
orphanage, a transition to a new family, language, culture, and a
mom who was fixated on her height would provide the grace needed
to survive an amputation in the future.

On the long ride home from the hospital, I prayed about my
heart. I had been searching for ways to "fix" Anna. I had harbored
a secret contract with God. I would bring her back to the USA and
he would provide a doctor who could "fix" her. The problem was
that Anna didn't need fixed. *I did.* And, with all my fears, grief,
and worries, I was missing a miracle.

My little girl was a walking miracle. Over twelve orthopedists
had confirmed it and I had missed it. There was no reason that she
could walk, and yet, every day, she jumped out of bed and did it.
Anna was a living, breathing, *walking* miracle. And, I, finally, was
really beginning to understand that.

We decided to wait. There was no need to amputate her foot as
long as she was able to walk. As we waited, I prayed diligently for
another answer. I grieved, I cried out to God, I raged at God for the
losses she faced. And, finally I submitted.

"If this is the path she's called down, then we'll help her." I
told God before the next orthopedic visit. "It's going to be such a
hard road, but at least she'll have a family to walk it with her."

We went to her next doctor's appointment with fear and dread
in our hearts. What would the doctor say? Would he give us a time
frame for how much longer she would be able to walk? All the

orthopedists agreed on one opinion: amputate the right foot. And, although it broke our hearts, we were ready to move forward with it.

God's provision and plan became clear that day.

"It's called a *prosthosis*, rather than prosthesis," her prosthetist explained. "It's because it encases her foot rather than replaces it."

Several weeks later, Anna, her hair in two braids, sporting purple overalls and a white flowered shirt, walked out our front door to go to art class with two feet touching the ground. God's answer came in the form of a "prosthotic" leg. While this prosthosis will never be her "real" foot, it encompasses and supports her foot while making her legs both the same length. And, though I didn't know it then, it would make it possible for Anna to run, play in the snow — even learn *tae kwon do*.

As I watched her walk out the door that day, I knew that God had made a way to save her foot. Finally, the miracle of her walking was not lost on me anymore.

As I wrestled with God over the issue of Anna's legs, I had a painful lesson that I had to learn. I was so angry that, despite my heartfelt prayers, he would not heal my daughter like he had Justin. The apostle Paul experienced this same grief, grief that comes when God, in his perfect wisdom, chooses not to remove a burden, but to leave that burden there to push you on to maturity and reveal his awesome power.

> *To keep me from becoming conceited ... there was given me a thorn in my flesh ... to torment me. Three times I pleaded with the Lord to take it away from me. But he said to me, "My grace is sufficient for you, for my power is made perfect in weakness." Therefore I will boast all the more gladly about my weaknesses, so that Christ's power may rest on me ... I delight in weaknesses ... in difficulties. For when I am weak, then I am strong.*
> — 2 Corinthians 12:7-10 (NIV)

That was my Anna. God's power made perfect in her weakness.

All Things New

Although the world is full of suffering, it is also full of the overcoming of it.

Faith is the strength by which a shattered world shall emerge into the light. — Helen Keller

When peace, like a river, attendeth my way,
When sorrows like sea billows roll;
Whatever my lot, Thou has taught me to say,
It is well, it is well, with my soul.
— Horatio G. Spafford

Therefore, if anyone is in Christ, he is a new creation; the old has gone, the new has come!
— 2 Corinthians 5:17 (NIV)

The thief cometh not, but for to steal, and to kill, and to destroy: I am come that they might have life, and that they might have it more abundantly.
— John 10:10 (NIV)

Anna noted every detail of our family life. Each day she made her bed, she noted that her brothers had something that she did not — a small decorative pillow, with a cross-stitched picture of a child that resembled the owner of the pillow. One day, she picked up Ben's pillow and began to study it.

"What does this say, Ben?" she asked, pointing at the letters.

"It says, 'Jesus loves Ben.' Grandma made it for me. She made one for all her grandkids."

Anna ran her fingers over the cross-stitch and hugged the pillow to her chest.

"It's a nice pillow," she replied.

Several months later, we drove to a restaurant three hours north of our home in order to pick up the boys after a visit to their grandparents. As we were packing the boys into the car, my mom approached Anna, her arms held behind her back.

"I have something for you, Anna," she said.

"I'll close my eyes and you can put it in my lap." Anna was always good at creating drama.

My mom gently set a pillow on Anna's lap. On the pillow was a cross-stitched picture of a girl with big brown eyes and honey blonde hair. Next to the picture were three words: Jesus loves Anna.

Anna's eyes opened, and she squealed with delight. Hugging the pillow tightly, she thanked her grandma.

"Oh! Jesus loves Anna! My own pillow! Thank you, Grandma! Jesus loves Anna! You made me one, too!"

And, without further ado, she launched into a loud rendition of "Jesus Loves Me," which she joyfully sang for the next hour and a half.

"She's grandchild number fourteen, but she's the first one to have such a reaction to their pillow." My mom smiled as she hugged Anna.

Anna understood something that those thirteen other grandchildren didn't understand. They didn't understand it because they had had a family their entire lives. What mattered was not the pillow itself, but what it represented. At the young age of three, she understood that she was being claimed as part of our family.

That spring, she had her first birthday party. Not a group party for all the children in her orphanage, but a celebration of her life. For days I planned the event and we invited all of our family and friends. It rained that day, and we had more people crammed into our house than could easily fit. Children ran all over the house, blowing bubbles and chasing each other. Anna opened more presents than she could mentally process and declared that the only cake in the world that she liked was her own birthday cake.

Later that day, we watched the video and I was once again moved by the changes in her life. The video camera panned around the room, showing cousins, aunts, uncles, grandparents, friends, brothers, and, finally me, holding Anna next to her cake. Then the large chorus of people began to sing their off-key rendition of "Happy Birthday," and Anna blew out the candles. In just about a year, Anna had gone from a child with no one to call her own, to a child with a family so large that they couldn't all fit into our house.

In the course of that year, God had knit her into our family. Learning English, grieving her losses, learning to trust, slaying *Baba Yaga*, and delighting in food, a warm home, and the love of a family were all part of that process of healing.

But just like the adoption was not easy or painless, neither was the process of healing and attaching. God worked through each pain, both hers and mine, and healed each one.

The ashes were taken away, and in their place he bestowed on her a crown of beauty when her faced filled out and the colors of her hair, eyes, and skin became bolder and more vivid from her dramatic change in diet. Her hair became her glory as it grew longer and longer and I brushed it and placed pretty bows and barrettes in it.

Her mourning was replaced by the oil of gladness, which came in the form of her brothers' love and joy and in the freedom she had gained to explore our neighborhood, the woods behind our house, and the creek in our neighbor's yard.

The spirit of despair was quickly replaced by the garment of praise when she rested in the truth that God brought her home and that he loved her, and as she was daily taught that truth by her mama, papa, family, and friends.

Over the year, she became like a giant oak of righteousness, a natural work of art, planted by the Lord himself, displaying his splendor and majesty and radiating his joy and hope. Full of energy and life, Anna's presence can literally light up a room and her life has offered many people hope. She became a miracle to behold.

Not long after her first anniversary home, during a viewing of the movie *Finding Nemo*, Anna whispered in my ear "Is the daddy fish going to give up?" Her first big screen experience, she gasped and marveled at each danger Marlin, the father fish, faced as he searched the ocean for his missing son, Nemo.

Her astonishment with the big screen and her concern over the plot continued until the climax of the movie, when Marlin and Nemo were reunited. As the fish swam toward each other, calling out their names, Anna threw her arm around my neck and squeezed me tightly.

"I knew that he wouldn't give up! Mommies and daddies never give up when they're looking for their kids. Just like you and daddy never gave up when you were looking for me!"

We did look for her until we found her. What we did for her, she could have never done for herself — not the paperwork, not the travel, not even the court appearance. She simply could not give herself a future. It took us to bridge the gap between her and home. We had to pay the money, do the paperwork, make the sacrifice, and fly to the other side of the world. It was a gulf she could simply not bridge.

She was rescued, but not by us. We're not "wonderful saints that rescued the poor orphan girl from across the world," but were merely the vessels that God used to accomplish his purpose, her redemption. Ours is a position of great honor, for we were able to see, firsthand, how great the love of God is. He is a God that will move heaven and earth simply out of love for one little girl.

Our family had the privilege of being witnesses of a word picture of that love. While we were still lost, abandoned, and simply waiting for someone to come, Jesus left his home in heaven to live on earth, just as we traveled to be with Anna. He paid the price for our salvation when he died on the cross. We suffered through an expensive, endless bureaucratic maze that split our family across the world. Then, he rescued us when he won the victory over death with his resurrection. He bridged a gap that we could not have ever bridged. We became children of the king, joint heirs with Jesus — just as a little orphan girl named Halyna became a beloved daughter named Anna.

What we did in our adoption was not charity. Each day, we live in the joy of being with Anna and having her as a part of our family. She is our sunshine, our light, and she helped to complete the design of our family. It is an understatement to say that we need her as much as she needs us. I have to believe that Jesus feels the same way about us: He takes joy in the relationships for which he sacrificed so much. Just as Anna was the reward for our work, *we* are his reward for his sacrifice.

We did look for Anna until we found her, for what else could we do? She was ours, and we could never leave her or forsake her — even when we didn't know her. And, with such fervent love, the God of orphans and widows pursues those who are ready to come home, and he will continue to look for them until he finds them because that is what a good daddy does.

There is so much of Anna's life we will never be able to explain. Why is this his plan? Why did God allow her to be born with a disability? Why her? Why would he choose not to display his power through her healing? Why would he allow years of needless suffering under the cruel reign of the Soviet Union? It's a list of questions that could continue infinitely, so instead, I stop and ask a different question: What next? And the answers to that are infinite as well. Paralympics? Horseback riding? Swimming? Driving? Soccer? Art lessons? Piano lessons? Drama classes? The ACT or the SAT? College at home or far away? Marriage? Children? There is no end to the list of possibilities and no way to know where God will lead her. It's those possibilities that I choose to celebrate.

There will always be a part of me that grieves over losses that are inherent in adoption and disabilities, but those unanswered questions and those losses are far outweighed by the joy of having her as my daughter. Therein lies the real blessings of following God's leading: Those who serve are as blessed as those who receive.

The thought that God had planted years ago when I taught my first piano student was true. There are unexpected blessings and joy when parenting a special-needs child. It is an entirely different kind of pride, and over the years I have experienced it again and again — her first jumps, learning to hop on one foot, sewing something, cutting (using her foot to hold the paper), learning to swim, and learning to play the piano. Each accomplishment has so much meaning as I look at the big picture of her life.

While it hasn't been easy, I wouldn't trade places with any other mother in the entire world.

Yet, as believers in Jesus, this idea shouldn't come as a surprise. The Bible is full of examples of God redeeming what was a hopeless situation and making it into something wonderful. Joseph, the son of Jacob, was betrayed by his brothers, sold into slavery, and unjustly imprisoned — only to save his family, the nation of Israel, and preserve the lineage of Jesus. Moses, destined to die at the hand of the Egyptians, was hidden by his birth mother, adopted into the family of Pharaoh, and ultimately led the Israelites out of slavery. The Israelites in Persia faced annihilation until they were redeemed by God through the acts of Esther. And, of course, Jesus was crucified on the cross and then overcame death through his resurrection. It's what our God does: makes beauty from ashes. If only we, as the body of Christ, would always live in anticipation of what beauty he'll create next!

Why does Anna have the disabilities that she has? Did God create her that way? It's a debate that's ongoing in the limb different community, and one that I would never profess to have the final answer. But I do know that God has been with Anna since the day that she was conceived. I also believe that Satan has always been terrified of who she can become in Christ. She has a heart that earnestly seeks to serve God and a bright intelligent spirit that fears little. She will always be a valiant warrior, and because of that passion, I believe that the attacks on her life started even before she was born. I also believe that God's counterattack and rescue began then as well, and clearly the side of righteousness has prevailed!

"Put your finger here; see my hands. Reach out your hand and put it into my side. Stop doubting and believe," Jesus told Thomas.

Days earlier, Thomas had said, "Unless I see the nail marks in his hands, and put my finger where the nails were, and put my hand into his side, I will not believe it."

As Nancy L. Eiesland points out in her book, *The Disabled God* (Nashville: Abingdon Press, 1994), Jesus, who could've returned with a perfect body, chose, instead, to return in a body disabled and marred by the wounds of his battle. His post-resurrection disability was his *choice*. Yet, this didn't make him less victorious but showed exactly how victorious he had been. There was no shame in his disfigurement. "Put your finger here." "Reach out your hand and put it into my side." These statements show forthrightness about the wounds, certainly not shame. His wounds, Anna's differences, they're all symbols of God's power made perfect in human weakness.

What was intended for evil was used for good, and what has been left is a body that is beautiful both in design and in intent. The issue is not whether God made Anna "that" way, but what God has done to redeem what could've been a life of sorrow. He took a person that had no life, no future, no hope, and he made her new. He made her beautiful.

Then he blessed me by inviting me to be a part of his plan.

Epilogue

"Who is that?" Ben asked as he peered over my shoulder reading my email. He pointed to a picture of a beautiful baby girl.

"A little girl in Kazakhstan," I replied. "We were sent her picture because this agency is looking for someone to adopt her."

"Can we?" he asked, a huge grin on his face. The ease of the question fully indicated that Ben did not comprehend all that was involved in not only adopting a baby from a different country, but also the subsequent years spent raising her. I thought of a million arguments why the answer should be "No." However, the problem was that I wanted the answer to be "Yes."

The little girl, named Saya, was of Kazakh descent, with large, brown eyes and beautiful wispy black hair. Her most prominent features were large, chubby cheeks that centered around a tiny nose and little lips. She looked like a perfect china doll, except for her hands. She was a waiting child because of severely deformed hands and forearms and a possible heart defect.

"Let's send the picture to Daddy, and see what he says...."

Before long, we decided to step out of the boat again. This time, though, the battle would be even bigger, and we soon came to learn that our time in Ukraine was simply training for the battle to redeem Saya's life. Although this adoption was longer, over twice as expensive, and involved much more travel, we stayed the course.

Why? Because each morning, we woke to hear a little girl singing, jumping, and dancing as she dressed and did her morning chores. And, each morning a beautiful little girl, her honey blonde hair shining and her brown eyes sparkling would slide down the steps and jump into my arms.

"Time for my good-morning hug!" And with that I would get my good morning hug and kiss from Anna.

For the rest of the day we could listen to non-stop chatter and answer 1,000 questions for our little girl.

"Where do birds go when it rains?"

"Why do people speak Russian so loudly?"

"I love dogs. Do dogs love me?"

And, in the evening as we tucked her in bed, we could answer the question that we loved the most: "Can you tell me again, the story about how you adopted me?"

So, we stuck with it and waited out the Kazakh government. In spring of 2004, Rob and I boarded a plane bound for Almaty, Kazakhstan, unsure of when we would be able to return. Eight weeks later, I exited the plane pushing a stroller that contained our newest family member: Saya Rachel Amend.

It was just like it was when I returned from Ukraine — only better. This time, I cried as I hugged my *three* children, and then began the introductions: "Anna, this is your new sister, Saya."

Anna smiled as she replied, "Welcome home, Saya."

Becoming Involved In Orphan Ministry

A religion that is pure and stainless according to God the Father is this: to take care of orphans and widows who are suffering, and to keep oneself unstained by the world. — James 1:27 (ISV)

Although not every family is called to adopt, every person who professes a faith in Jesus is called to serve the orphan and the widow. Adoption is one way to enjoy the blessings and miracles of serving the orphan, but God has also opened up other ways.

Offer Your Money As A Gift
To Ministries That Work With Orphans

The number one way to help orphans is to give money to families in the adoption process. Sometimes the donation of frequent flier miles, hotel perks, or other travel aids can be very useful. Help with meals and child care is a significant way to help, too.

There are also many wonderful ministries that serve orphans through practical services such as providing food, clothing, toys, diapers, and other necessary supplies, some provide medical care, and some help other families adopt waiting children. Listed on the following pages are some organizations that work zealously to serve orphaned children.

The Shepherd's Crook

The Shepherd's Crook Ministries
P.O. Box 773
West Chester, Ohio 45071
Phone: 513-844-8873
www.theshepherdscrook.org

The Shepherd's Crook is a ministry that serves the neediest orphans around the world. They accomplish their mission through both adoption support to families (although they are not an adoption agency), and through medical mission trips — where often a doctor will travel with a team of nurses to not only perform surgeries in impoverished nations, but to teach the doctors there as well. They also offer practical support to orphanages around the world.

My Home

MASTER Provisions
ATTN: My Home
1769 Promontory Drive
Florence, Kentucky 41042
www.masterprovisions.org

My Home, a ministry of MASTER Provision, provides support to Christian Ukrainian families that adopt orphans or street children. For just a small amount of money, a family in the US could make it possible for a Ukrainian orphan to be adopted into a loving Christian family!

Shaohannah's Hope
Shaohannah's Hope
P.O. Box 647
Franklin, Tennessee 37065
Phone: 615-550-5600
Fax: 615-595-0850
www.shaohannahshope.org
   This ministry, started by Stephen Curtis Chapman and his family is a great resource for helping both orphans and families hoping to adopt. Opportunities for donating to grants, building special orphanages for medically needy children, and other special projects abound. Donations should be made out to Shaohannah's Hope.

Frontier Horizon
Frontier Horizon
P.O. Box 4429
Virginia Beach, Virginia 23454
www.frontierhorizon.org
   Frontier Horizon is a humanitarian aid organization that organizes hosting trips for older waiting orphans to spend time in the United States with a family during the summer. While many of the children are available for adoption, Frontier Horizon is not an adoption agency and the purpose of hosting the children is to provide opportunities to expand these children's horizons. This is a large (and expensive) commitment, but can also be phenomenally rewarding. Older children need families just as much as the younger ones! This is also an excellent way to "get your feet wet" if you're considering adoption of an older child, but not yet ready to commit.

Gift of Adoption
Nataliya Khomyak
SHB 325
977 Centerville Turnpike
Virginia Beach, VA 23463
www.emmanuil.tv/english/adoption-project.htm

Gift of Adoption is a ministry of the Christian Broadcast Network. Working in Ukraine, CBN is known as Mission Emmanuel and broadcasts Christian shows on Ukrainian television. Gift of Adoption grew out of the network's desire to serve the orphans of Ukraine, beyond their work of simply providing compelling stories about both the orphan's needs and Christians who have risen to the call of serving them. Gift of Adoption helps select families facilitate the adoptions of waiting children, provides educational trips to the United States for older orphans, and, as a main focus of ministry, partners orphans that have been phased out of the orphanage system with Ukrianian families that can support them as they try to learn how to survive in their society, further their education, find legitimate jobs and simply not be alone and vulnerable. Donations can be made to the Christian Broadcast Network. Mark "Gift of Adoption" in the memo and mail to Natalia Khomyak.

His Kids, Too!
His Kids, Too!
PMB #180, 3491 Thomasville Rd.
Tallahassee, Florida 32309
Phone: 850-524-5437 (KIDS)
www.hiskidstoo.org
Focusing on the eastern European country of Ukraine, His Kids, Too! is committed to unconditionally sharing the love of Jesus Christ to orphans, widows, and those in need through providing food, medicine, clothing, and other supplies; teaching godly principals; education opportunities; and offering adoption assistance.

Started by an adoptive mom, His Kids, Too! began by serving three orphanages, and now serves over 5,000 children!

Although not specifically adoption related, donating money to organizations such as these, can very well prevent a large number of children from becoming orphans:

World Vision
World Vision
P.O. Box 9716, Dept. W
Federal Way, Washington 98063-9716
Phone: 1-888-511-6548
www.worldvision.org
   World Vision offers opportunities, for a small monthly fee, to sponsor children and provide food, clothing, and an education.

The Heifer Project
Heifer Project International
1 World Avenue
Little Rock, Arkansas 72202
Phone: 1-800-422-0474
www.heifer.org
   The Heifer Project serves impoverished people by providing live food for them. When donating to the Heifer project, a person chooses from their catalogue what animals to purchase — anything from a small flock of chickens to dairy cattle are available. There are also opportunities to purchase equipment used to help people start small businesses.

Samaritan's Purse
Samaritan's Purse
P.O. Box 3000
Boone, North Carolina 28607
Phone: 828-262-1980
Fax: 828-266-1026
www.samaritanspurse.org
   Samaritan's Purse provides relief and development opportunities in impoverished parts of the world. In addition to Operation Christmas Child, they also provide medical care, specifically a program that helps children with life-threatening medical conditions. They also have ministries addressing the HIV/AIDS problem — something that is currently impacting the number of orphans in Africa.

Organize An Orphan Ministry At Your Church

Through one of the above ministries, you can organize a sponsoring and prayer program for specific orphans.

Support adoptive families within your church and community by offering free child care or respite nights, meals, and even financial gifts.

Organize missions trips that include orphanage service — a word of caution though. Many orphanages welcome people from missions trips, but do so in the hope that people will see the children and want to adopt. If you do a short-term mission trip to an orphanage, remember that these children will still be facing the same future when you go home. And, no matter how emotional, don't make promises that you'll come back unless you truly intend to come back.

Find Ways To Support Your Local Foster System

Foster parents often need times of respite, but often cannot just leave children in their care with friends or family. Many county foster systems are looking for people willing to provide respite care for children in the foster system. After being certified as a respite care provider, a person can provide anywhere from an evening of babysitting, to several days of care so that a foster family is free to have a night out without the kids or to take a vacation out of state.

Call the local foster system and find out the specific needs of the system. Oftentimes when children are removed from an abusive home, they leave with nothing but the clothes on their backs. Caring Christians can fill in those gaps by providing bags with hygiene items, small toys, snacks, stuffed animals, or blankets for comfort.

Many court systems have a Guardian ad Litem or Court Appointed Special Advocate (CASA) program. It takes a serious amount of training to become a CASA, however the impact that you can have on the life of a child is tremendous. As a CASA you will most likely be the most consistent person in the life of a child caught in the foster system. A child who might leave and return to their birth family multiple times and go through several foster families will often have the same guardian ad litem for their entire childhood.

A CASA not only functions as the eyes and ears of the court system (seeing what life is like in the foster home) but also can advocate for the child to receive much needed therapy, academic assistance, or even physical needs that might be present for a child aging out of the foster system.

Remember that we, the church, are the body of Christ here on earth. If we don't rise to the call of serving these children, then who will? The blessings will far outweigh the sacrifice.

A Brief Guide To Adoption

Common Adoption Myths

People don't love adopted children like they do their biological children. It's just not the same.

This is probably the most common adoption myth, and it is just that: a myth. When you adopt a child that child belongs to you, he is your child just as though you gave birth to him. As a mother of biological and adopted children, I can attest to the fact that neither way of building a family is superior — they are simply different. Once the children are in your family, it no longer matters how they got there.

Adopted children have more problems than birth children.

While the transition period after adoption can be difficult, adopted children have a great success rate in life. Unfortunately, the media tends to focus its attention on the more difficult situations. The reality, which is backed up by research rather than television dramas, is that adopted children are just as likely as birth children to struggle or be successful in life.

Adoption is always extremely expensive.

"Not when you're taking a child off the hands of the county!" an adoptive mom once told me — and indeed she is correct. In most cases, foster-to-adopt through the county government is not only cheap, but free. Also, there is often continuing help with medical issues, therapy, and such even after the adoption is completed.

There are often grants for adopting waiting children from orphanages, as well as the federal tax credit, which allows most families to recoup up to $10,000 of adoption expenses over the course of five years. Using cheap airfare or frequent flier miles (which can be donated to you) can also significantly bring down the cost of an international adoption.

Most families that adopt, both domestically or internationally, are middle class families, not wealthy, so obviously there must be a great discrepancy in the amount of money an adoption costs.

In a culture where we routinely spend $20,000 on a new car, over $1,000 to send a daughter to prom, and take annual vacations, spending $15,000 to save the life of a child really shouldn't be an issue.

Adoption is the same thing as buying a baby.

NO! If a family buys a baby they pay the birthmother and/or some type of broker for the baby. Oftentimes there will be false paperwork involved. Buying a baby is completely unethical and totally illegal for a myriad of reasons.

Legitimate adoption expense covers the following items:

- fees for services such as a translator, lawyer filing and handling paperwork, an agency that is identifying and helping to support a child;
- lodging fees while in country;
- airfare;
- immigration fees;
- home study fee;
- court fees;
- post-adoption social worker visits and paperwork;
- maternity care (in the US); and
- fees for foster care while your child waits for you.

With adoption, you become that child's parent not because you paid someone money, but because the governing authorities in that child's life have legally deemed that they are yours.

Your birth children will resent you bringing strangers into your home.

Would your birth children resent it if you birthed another baby into your family? In our experience, our children have always been happy to welcome another sibling and have never thought anything different than that the new child was their new sibling.

If bonding doesn't happen by age three, then your child will have attachment disorder.

Although Reactive Attachment Disorder (RAD) is a true psychological issue (and one that is a growing concern in the US not because of adoption but because of the large number of children spending more and more hours in daycare and subsequently losing bonding time with parents), it is actually quite rare. In the cases where it does occur, there are treatments and therapies that exist to help teach the child to attach. If the problem occurs, it is not something that can just be conquered by "love" but will need to be addressed with the help of professionals and a good support network for the family.

That said, what research has shown is that the important thing for a child is that they attach to someone while in the orphanage. If they can attach to a particular caregiver, or even a few caregivers, then once adopted they can transfer that attachment to their new parents.

Attachment doesn't happen overnight. It's a process that happens as you and your child grow in your relationship and your child grieves the relationships that she has lost due to the adoption. At the same time, she will be going through the normal phases of childhood where she'll be wanting more independence — while still trying to attach. The amazing thing, though, is you get to see and experience that attachment happening in a much more vivid and expedited manner than how it happens with a newborn.

183

Is God Calling You To Adopt?

If you believe that God is calling you to adopt, then he probably is. However, there are some issues you need to consider while hearing that call.

Is your spouse in agreement with you about the calling?

Adoption absolutely should not happen unless both spouses are committed to it 100%. If you feel called by God to adopt and your spouse doesn't, then for now, your focus should be prayer. Talk with your spouse about it, but don't nag. Ask if he is willing to take a period of time, perhaps a week or a month, and pray before talking again. If your spouse is consistently against the idea, then it will have to prayerfully wait until you are both on board with the idea.

How emotionally healthy is your family?

While no family is perfect, it is important that your family be emotionally healthy. Just like adding a newborn means more stress, adopting a child adds stress to a family. If there are marital problems, significant behavior or emotional problems with your children, or unusually high stress levels, then you should solve those issues first and then move toward adoption.

Is he calling you to do this right now?

How old are your birth children? Is God preparing your heart for an adoption down the road, when your birth children are a bit older? Is God calling you to wait so that you can adopt an older child? The call doesn't have to mean to act now.

A General Explanation Of The Adoptive Process

Once you and your spouse have decided that God is calling you to adopt, the next question becomes, "Where do we begin?"

The answers to that will vary from state to state, and will also depend upon what type of adoption God is calling you to. In general, though, the process would go like this:

1. Research the type of adoptions that exist and determine where God is leading you. Your options are, basically:

    *   international adoption from an orphanage or foster care,
    *   domestic infant adoption through a private agency, and/or
    *   foster-to-adopt through your county's Job and Family Services.

    There are also differences within domestic private adoption regarding an identified adoption, where the birthmother knows you and picks you, adopting through an agency where birthparents select your file from the agency or many other specific options that can be based upon those scenarios. There are also open adoptions (where there is communication with the birth family) and closed (no communication with the birth family or even knowledge of the birth family). Right now, in the US, it is much more common to hear of open private infant adoptions than ever before.

2. If you decided to go with an adoption through the county, then most likely you will attend a series of classes presented by them, go through a home study, and then wait for placement.

3. If you choose to go international, then you must decide what country you wish to adopt from. Every country has different adoption laws. To help you decide first find out which countries you qualify to adopt from. Issues that would hinder qualification would be: age, income, health issues, and marital status. Then determine which countries have an adoption program that would work for your family. For instance, some countries, like Ukraine, require lengthy stays. Some countries, like the Philippines, require a short trip, and some countries, like Korea or Ethiopia, will escort your new child to the US.

4. While deciding on a country, you must also find an international agency that will serve that country. You must meet their requirements as well, which are often the same as the country requirements but can vary.

5. If you choose an international agency that is not located in your area, you will also need to locate a local adoption agency that can perform your home study.

6. Once all that is decided the paperwork will begin. Your paperwork will have to satisfy three governing authorities:

   • state government;
   • US federal government; and
   • your child's foreign government.

   You'll start your paperwork with the home study.

7. The home study process will generally last about four to six months for your first adoption. There will be required classes to attend, a slew of personal information paperwork, and another slew of legal paperwork and background checks.

8. As you complete the home study, you can also file your Orphan Petition and begin the lengthy process of immigration. Your home study and international agency will be able to help you with this.

9. After the home study is complete, you will then begin to compile a dossier of papers that will need to be submitted to the country you wish to adopt from. This dossier will include:

   • your final home study;
   • proof of immigration filing;
   • financial statements;
   • background checks; and
   • medical information.

Every country requires different papers, and some countries require the papers to all be not only notarized by but also authenticated by the US State Department or "Apostilled" by your state's Secretary of State.

10.   The dossier will then be sent, probably through your agency, to a translator in your child's country. It will be translated and then submitted for approval to that country's government. At this point, you will wait and possibly begin to prepare for your trip.

11.   Once you are approved, then you will be given a travel date, and you will travel to complete whatever adoption process that country requires.

12.   After arriving home with your new child, you will probably need to have several post-placement visits with a social worker, and you will need to complete the process of verifying the child's citizenship. There is also a process called "re-adoption" which is highly recommended, but not always necessary. With re-adoption, a county judge will rule that your adoption is legal and place your county's stamp of approval on the adoption. Your child will then receive a local birth certificate listing you as his parents. This paper will be helpful to your child when entering school or at any other time they need to use a birth certificate.

Resources
http://travel.state.gov/family/adoption/adoption_485.html
The US State Department website is an excellent place to start your research on countries to adopt from.

You can access the adoption laws of every country you may be interested in adopting from, as well as see an overview of the adoption process for that country. Of course, adoption laws do change, so check each page to see when it was last updated.

www.adoption.com

This website is a clearinghouse of information on adoption — all types of adoption. This is a great resource for someone still trying to decide what type of adoption will work for their family.

www.adoptive.families.com

This website is connected with the popular and informative magazine, *Adoptive Families,* and offers articles from the magazine, adoption guides, and links to information that will help adoptive families once the child is home.

www.tapestrybooks.com

This website is a catalogue of adoption books and provides the opportunity to purchase not only books to help families through the adoption process and after the adoption process, but also books for children, as well.